AF553765

ENCYCLOPAEDIA OF SCHOOL EDUCATION

Vol. III

SUCCESSFUL SCHOOLING

By

Dr. Digumarti Bhaskara Rao
M.Sc., M.A., M.A., M.Ed., Ph.D.
Principal
R.V.R. College of Education
D-43 (277) S.V.N. Colony
Guntur - 522 006 (India)

DISCOVERY PUBLISHING HOUSE PVT. LTD.
NEW DELHI-110 002

Reprinted - 2016

ISBN: 978-81-7141-677-6

Successful Schooling

Published by:

DISCOVERY PUBLISHING HOUSE PVT. LTD.
4383/4B, Ansari Road, Darya Ganj
New Delhi-110 002 (India)
Phone: +91-11-23279245, 43596064-65
Fax: +91-11-23253475
E-mail: discoverypublishinghouse@gmail.com
sales@discoverypublishinggroup.com
web: www.discoverypublishinggroup.com

Printed at:
Infinity Imaging Systems
Delhi

PREFACE

School is a formal place where a prescribed curriculum is imparted by the teachers during a definite duration of time. A well-conducted school is a happy home, a social centre, a recreation place, a body building stadium, and a workshop. A good school meets the individual requirements, provides activity-oriented learning experiences, builds an all-round personality, develops social and personal values, prepares for practical life, produces civic citizens, encourages corporate life, develops cultural pluralism, perpetuates society, propagates ideologies of the state, realises the goals of education, preserves and transmits culture, develops mental powers, brings emotional stability, promotes good character, builds physique, etc. The society along with individuals cannot prosper without proper schooling. Thats why, a school must be conducted in a successful way.

Considering the importance of successful schooling, this book, 'Successful Schooling', is prepared selecting the best suited topics. Each chapter explains first the research findings of the concerned concept and later provides the suggestions suitable for application. By understanding each concept concretely, any administrator can successfully conduct the school activities, any teacher can successfully teach the subject matter, any parent can successfully meet the child's requirements, and any educationist can successfully develop suitable educational programmes.

I am thankful to the authors; the Director, International Bureau of Education, UNESCO, Geneva, Switzerland, the President, International Academy of Education, Brussels,

Belgium, and the Director-General, United Nations Educational Scientific and Cultural Organisation, Paris, France for utilising their contributions and publications in preparing this book for the benefit of educational planners and administrators, curriculum designers and authors, teachers and taught, and parents.

As schools are no longer just places where children acquire education, it is the responsibility of all concerned to successfully conduct the schools.

Bhaskara Rao

CONTENTS

Preface

1. Effective Educational Practices 1
2. How Children Learn? 16
3. Teaching 34
4. Tutoring 59
5. Teaching Additional Languages 85
6. Motivation to Learn 101
7. Preventing Behaviour Problems: *What Works?* 121
8. Wasted Opportunities When Schools Fail 142

Bibliography *199*

1

Effective Educational Practices

*Herbert J. Walberg**
*Susan J. Paik***

Introduction

The educational practices described in this chapter can generally be applied to classroom subjects in primary and secondary schools. They show large, positive learning effects for students in widely varying conditions. Educators may find the many references valuable in investigating the applicability of the practices in their particular circumstances. As with all educational practices, of course, they can be effectively or ineffectively planned and conducted, and the results may vary accordingly.

The research on these practices has accumulated over half a century. Several of the major references used are studies conducted by my colleagues and myself. These studies compiled the results of research summaries and synthesized several hundred investigations of educational practices by many scholars. The practices were further investigated by analysing large national and international achievement surveys. Much of the research employed examinations covering the facts and principles

* University of Illinois at Chicago, United States of America.
** University of Illinois at Chicago, United States of America.

of the usual or predominant academic subjects. The research is less pertinent to art, music and athletics, subjects that may have a more behavioural and less academic emphasis. Nor did the research concentrate on such aspects of learning as writing, problem-solving and completing laboratory projects. Research on these subjects and skills may be found in the references and elsewhere.

As mentioned above, the practices in this booklet are generally powerful and consistent in promoting important aspects of academic learning. Some other practices are nearly as good.

Parent Involvement

Learning is enhanced when schools encourage parents to stimulate their children's intellectual development.

Research Findings

Dozens of studies have shown that the home environment has a powerful effect on what children and youth learn within and outside school. This environment is considerably more powerful than the parents' income and education in influencing what children learn in the first six years of life and during the twelve years of primary and secondary education. One major reason that parental influence is so strong is that, from infancy until the age of 18, children spend approximately 92 per cent of their time outside school under the influence of their parents.

Co-operative efforts by parents and educators to modify these alterable academic conditions in the home have strong, beneficial effects on learning. In twenty-nine controlled studies, 91 per cent of the comparisons favoured children in such programmes over non-participant control groups.

In the Classroom

Sometimes called 'the curriculum of the home', the home environment refers to informed parent/child conversations about school and everyday events; encouragement and discussion of leisure reading; monitoring and critical review of television viewing and peer activities; deferral of immediate gratification to accomplish long-term goals; expressions of affection and interest in the child's academic and other progress as a person; and perhaps, among such unremitting efforts, laughter and caprice. Reading to children and discussing everyday events prepare them for academic activities before attending school.

Co-operation between educators and parents can support these approaches. Educators can suggest specific activities likely to promote children's learning at home and in school. They can also develop and organise large-scale teacher/parent programmes to promote academically stimulating conditions and activities outside the school in a systematic manner.

Graded Homework

Students learn more when they complete homework that is graded, commented upon and discussed by their teachers.

Research Findings

A synthesis of more than a dozen studies of the effects of homework in various subjects showed that the assignment and completion of homework yield positive effects on academic achievement. The effects are almost tripled when teachers take time to grade the work, make corrections and specific comments on improvements that can be made, and discuss problems and solutions with individual students or the whole class. Homework also seems particularly effective in secondary school.

In the Classroom

Among developed countries, the United States has the least number of school days because of the long summer vacation. Students also spend less time, on average, doing homework. Extending homework time is a proven way to lengthen study time and increase achievement, although the quality of the assignments and of the completed work are also important.

Like a three-legged stool, homework requires a teacher to assign it and provide feedback, a parent to monitor it and a student to do it. If one leg is weak, the stool may fall down. The role of the teacher in providing feedback—in reinforcing what has been done correctly and in re-teaching what has not—is the key to maximizing the positive impact of homework.

Districts and schools that have well-known homework policies for daily minutes of required work are likely to reap benefits. Homework 'hotlines' in which students may call in for help have proved useful. To relieve some of the workload of grading, teachers can employ procedures in which students grade their own and other students' work. In this way, they can learn co-operative social skills and how to evaluate their own and others' efforts.

The quality of homework is as important as the amount. Effective homework is relevant to the lessons to be learned and in keeping with students abilities.

ALIGNED TIME ON TASK

Students who are actively focused on educational goals do best in mastering the subject matter.

Research Findings

More than 130 studies support the obvious idea that the more students study, the more they learn. It is one of the most consistent findings in all educational research. Time alone, however, does not suffice. Learning activities should reflect educational goals. This alignment or co-ordination of means with goals can be called 'curricular focus'. A similar reform term is 'systemic reform', which means that the three components of the curriculum—(1) goals, (2) textbooks, materials and learning activities, and (3) tests and other outcome assessments—are well matched in content and emphasis.

In the Classroom

The amount learned reflects both study time and curricular focus. Curricular focus represents efforts to decide what should be learned by a given age or grade level, and then concentrating attention, time and energy on these elements. Consequently, students at a given grade level should have greater degrees of shared knowledge and skills as prerequisites for further learning; teachers may then avoid excessive review; and progress can be better assessed.

Teachers have the most direct role in ensuring that this emphasis is carried into the classroom. The teacher's skilful classroom management, by taking into account what is to be learned and identifying the most efficient ways to present it, increases effective study time. Students who are actively engaged in activities focused on specific instructional goals make more progress towards these goals.

Direct Teaching

Direct teaching is most effective when it exhibits key features and follows systematic steps.

Research Findings

Many studies show that direct teaching can be effective in promoting student learning. The process emphasizes systematic sequencing of lessons, a presentation of new content and skills, guided student practice, the use of feedback and independent practice by students. The traits of teachers employing effective direct instruction include clarity, task orientation, enthusiasm and flexibility. Effective direct teachers also clearly organise their presentations and occasionally use student ideas.

In the Classroom

The use of direct teaching can be traced to the turn of the last century; it is what many citizens and parents expect to see in classrooms. Done well, it can yield consistent and substantial results. Whole-class teaching of diverse groups may mean that lessons are too advanced for slower students and too repetitive for the quick. In the last decade or two, moreover, theorists have tried to transfer more control of lesson planning and completion to students themselves so that they 'learn to learn', as several subsequent practices exemplify.

Six phased functions of direct teaching work well:

1. daily review, homework check and, if necessary, reteaching;
2. presentation of new content and skills in small steps;
3. guided student practice with close teacher monitoring;

4. corrective feedback and instructional reinforcement;
5. independent practice in work at the desk and in homework with a high (more than 90 per cent) success rate; and
6. weekly and monthly reviews.

ADVANCE ORGANISERS

Showing students the relationships between past learning and present learning increases its depth and breadth.

Research Findings

More than a dozen studies have shown that, when teachers explain how new ideas in the current lesson relate to ideas in previous lessons and other prior learning, students can connect the old with the new, which helps them to better remember and understand. Similarly, altering them to the learning of key-points allows them to concentrate on the most crucial parts of the lessons.

In the Classroom

Advance organisers help students focus on key ideas by enabling them to anticipate which points are important to learn. Understanding the sequence or continuity of subject-matter development, moreover, can be motivating. If students simply learn one isolated idea after another, the subject-matter may appear arbitrary. Given a 'mental road map' of what they have accomplished, where they are presently, and where they are going can avoid unpleasant surprises and help them to set realistic goals. Similar effects can be accomplished by goal-setting, overviewing and pre-testing before lessons that sensitize students to important points and questions that they will encounter in textbooks and will be presented by teachers.

It may also be useful to show how what is being learned solves problems that exist in the world outside school and that students are likely to meet in life. For example, human biology that features nutrition and its implications for food choices is likely to be more interesting than abstract biology.

Teachers and textbooks can sometimes make effective use of graphic advance organisers. Maps, timetables, flow charts depicting the sequence of activities, and other such devices may be worth hundreds of words. They may also be easier to remember.

The Teaching of Learning Strategies

Giving students some choice in their learning goals and teaching them to be attentive to their progress yield learning gains.

Research Findings

In the 1980s, cognitive research on teaching sought ways to encourage self-monitoring, self-teaching or 'meta-cognition' to foster achievement and independence. Skills are important, but the learner's monitoring and management of his or her own learning have primacy. This approach transfers part of the direct teaching functions of planning, allocating time and review to learners. Being aware of what goes on in one's mind during learning is a critical first step to effective independent learning.

Some students have been found to lack this self-awareness and must be taught the skills necessary to monitor and regulate their own learning. Many studies have demonstrated that positive effects can accrue from developed skills.

In the Classroom

Students with a repertoire of learning strategies can measure their own progress towards explicit goals. When students use these strategies to strengthen their opportunities for learning, they simultaneously increase their skills of self-awareness, personal control, and positive self-evaluation.

Three possible phases of teaching about learning strategies include:

1. modelling, in which the teacher exhibits the desired behaviour;
2. guided practice, in which students perform with help from the teacher; and

3. application, during which students act independently of the teacher.

As an example, a successful programme of 'reciprocal teaching' fosters reading comprehension by having students take turns in leading dialogues on pertinent features of texts. By assuming the roles of planning and monitoring ordinarily exercised by teachers, students learn self-management. Perhaps that is why tutors learn from tutoring, and why it is said: 'To learn something well, teach it'.

TUTORING

Teaching one student or a small number with the same abilities and instructional needs can be remarkably effective.

Research Findings

Tutoring gears learning to student needs. It has yielded large learning effects in several dozen studies. It yields particularly large effects in mathematics—perhaps because of the subject's well-defined sequence and organisation. If students fall behind in a fast-paced mathematics class, they may never catch up unless their particular problems are identified and remedied. This individualized assessment and follow-up process is the virtue of tutoring and other means of adaptive instruction.

In the Classroom

Peer tutoring (tutoring of slower or younger students by more advanced students) appears to work nearly as well as teacher tutoring; with sustained student practice it might be equal to teacher tutoring in some cases. Significantly, peer tutoring promotes effective learning in tutors as well as tutees. The need to organise one's thoughts in order to impart them intelligibly to others, the need to become conscious of the value of time, and the need to learn managerial and social skills are probably the main reasons for benefits to the tutor.

Even slower-learning students and those with disabilities can be in the position of teaching to others if they are given the extra time and practice that may be required to master a skill. This can give them a positive experience and increase their feelings to self-esteem. The success of two other practices in this booklet—the teaching of learning strategies and co-operative learning—is attributable to instructional features similar to those of tutoring.

MASTERY LEARNING

For subject-matter to be learned step by step, thorough mastery of each step is often optimal.

Research Findings

More than fifty studies show that careful sequencing, monitoring and control of the learning process raise the learning rate. Pre-testing helps determine what should be studied; this allows the teacher to avoid assigning material that has already been mastered or for which the student does not yet have the pre-requisite skills. Ensuring that students achieve mastery of initial steps in the sequence helps ensure that they will make satisfactory progress in subsequent, more advanced steps. Frequent assessment of progress informs teachers and students when additional time and corrective remedies are needed. Mastery learning appears to work best when the subject-matter is well organised.

In the Classroom

Because of its emphasis on outcomes and careful monitoring of progress, mastery learning can save learners' time. It allows more time and remediation for students who need it. It also enables faster learners to skip material they already know. Since mastery learning suits instruction to the needs of each student, it can work better than giving the whole class the same lesson at the same time. Such whole-class teaching may be too hard for some learners and too easy for others.

Mastery learning programmes require special planning, materials and producers. Teachers must be prepared to identify the components of instruction, develop assessment strategies so that individual students are appropriately placed in the instructional continuum, and provide reinforcement and corrective feedback—while continuously engaging students in lessons.

CO-OPERATIVE LEARNING

Students in small, self-instructing groups can support and increase each other's learning.

Research Findings

As shown by more than fifty studies, learning proceeds more effectively than useful when exchanges among teachers and learners are frequent and specifically directed towards students' problems and interests. In whole-class instruction, only one person can speak at a time, and shy or slow-learning students may be reluctant to speak at all. When students work in groups of two to four, however, each group member can participate extensively, individual problems are more likely to become clear and to be remedied (sometimes with the teacher's assistance), and learning can accelerate.

In the Classroom

With justification, co-operative learning has become widespread. Not only can it increase academic achievement, but also it has other virtues. By working in small groups, students learn teamwork, how to give and receive criticism, and how to plan, monitor and evaluate their individual and joint activities with others.

It appears that modern workplaces increasingly require such partial delegation of authority, group management and co-operative skills. Like modern managers, teachers may need to become more like facilitators, consultants and evaluators, rather than supervisors. Nonetheless, researchers do not recommend that co-operative learning take up the whole school day; the use of a variety of procedures, rather than co-operative learning alone, is considered to be most productive.

In addition, co-operative learning means more than merely assigning children to small groups. Teachers must also carefully design and prepare for the small-group setting. Students need instruction in skills necessary to operate successfully in small groups. Decisions must be made about the use of individual or group accountability. Care must be taken in establishing the mix of strengths and needs represented by students in the groups. Attention to these details will increase the likelihood that the co-operative groups will produce increased learning.

Adaptive Education

A variety of instructional techniques adapting lessons to individual students and small groups raises achievement.

Research Findings

Adaptive instruction is an integrated diagnostic-prescriptive process that combines several of the preceding practices—tutoring, mastery and co-operative learning, and instruction in learning strategies—into a classroom management system to tailor instruction to individual and small-group needs. The achievement effects of adaptive programmes have been demonstrated. The broader effects of adaptive instruction are probably underestimated, since it aims at diverse ends that are difficult to measure, including student autonomy, intrinsic motivation, teacher and student choice and parental involvement.

In the Classroom

Adaptive education requires implementation steps executed by a master teacher, including planning, time allocation, task delegation to aides and students, and quality control. Unlike most other practices, it is a comprehensive programme for the whole school day, rather than a single method that requires simple integration into one subject or into a single teacher's repertoire. Its focus on the individual student requires that barriers to learning are first diagnosed and then a plan developed to address those needs.

A student with special needs or experiencing academic difficulties becomes the shared responsibility of a team of teachers and specialists. Such an approach to education calls for teachers to develop a broad spectrum of teaching approaches, along with knowledge of when to use each of them most productively, and to co-ordinate their efforts with those of other professionals providing support to a student. Time and opportunity to do this are crucial for implementation of adaptive education.

Skilful professional management is required to integrate all aspects of the programme. For example, curricular co-ordination means more than a plan for the teaching of subject-matter skills and knowledge across grade levels as it applies to *all* students. Instead, it encompasses the relationship of that curriculum to the abilities and needs of *each* student. Consequently, central-office staff, principals and teachers need more than usual training to install and maintain adaptive programmes.

As goals for school become more clear and uniform, it should be increasingly possible to develop and employ systematic approaches, such as adaptive education.

REFERENCES

Anderson, L.W.; Walberg, H.J. 1994. *Time Piece: Extending and Enhancing Learning Time*. Reston, VA, National Association of Secondary School Principals.

Ausubel, D.P. 1968. *Educational Psychology: A Cognitive View*. New York, Holt, Rinehart and Winston.

Bloom, B.S. 1988. Helping All Children Learn Well in Elementary School—and Beyond. *Principal* (Alexandria, VA), Vol. 67, No. 4, p. 12-17.

Brophy J.; Good, T. 1986. Teacher-Effects Results. *In:* Wittrock, M.C., ed. *Handbook of Research on Teaching*. New York, Macmillan.

Cohen, P.A.; Kulik, J.A.; Kulik, C.L. 1982. Educational Outcomes of Tutoring: A Meta-Analysis of Findings. *American Educational Research Journal* (Washington, DC), Vol. 19, No. 2, p. 237-48.

Ehly, S.W. 1980. *Peer Tutoring for Individualized Instruction*. Boston, MA, Allyn and Bacon.

Fredrick, W.C. 1980. Instructional Time. *Evaluation in Education: An International Review Series* (Elmsford, NY), Vol. 4, p. 148-58.

Fredrick, W.C.; Walberg. H.J. 1980. Learning as a Function of Time. *Journal of Educational Research* (Washington, DC), Vol. 73, p. 183-94.

Gage, N.L.; Needles, M.C. 1989. Process-Product Research on Teaching. *Elementary School Journal* (Chicago, IL), Vol. 89, p. 253-300.

Graue, M.E.; Weinstein, T.; Walberg, H.J. 1983. School-based Home Reinforcement Programmes: A Quantitative Synthesis. *Journal of Educational Research* (Washington, DC), Vol. 76, p. 351-60.

Guskey, T.R. 1990. Cooperative Mastery Learning Strategies. *Elementary School Journal* (Chicago, IL), Vol. 91, No. 1, p. 33-42.

Haller, E.; Child, D.; Walberg, H.J. 1988. Can Comprehension be Taught? A Quantitative Synthesis. *Educational Researcher* (Washington, DC), Vol. 17, No. 9, p. 5-8.

Hertz-Lazarowitz, R.; Miller, N., eds. 1992. *Interaction in Co-operative Groups*. New York, Cambridge University Press.

Husén, T.; Postlethwaite, T.N., eds. 1994. *International Encyclopaedia of Education*. 2nd ed. Oxford, UK, Elsevier Science.

Iverson, B.K.; Walberg, H.J. 1982. Home Environment and Learning: A Quantitative Synthesis. *Journal of Experimental Education* (Boulder, CO), Vol. 50, p. 144-51.

Johnson, D.W.; Jhonson, R. 1989. *Co-operation and Competition: Theory and Research*. Edina, MN, Interaction Book Co.

Kulik, J.A.; Kulik, C.L.; Bangert-Drowns, R.L. 1990. Effectiveness of Mastery Learning Programmes: A Meta-Analysis. *Review of Educational Research*, (Washington, DC), Vol. 60, No. 2, p. 265-99.

Lipsey, M.W.; Wilson, D.B. 1993. The Efficacy of Psychological, Educational, and Behavioural Treatment: Confirmation from Meta-Analysis. *American Psychologist* (Washington, DC), Vol. 49, p. 1181-209.

Medway, F.J. 1991. A Social Psychological Analysis of Peer Tutoring. *Journal of Developmental Education* (Boone, NC), Vol. 15, No. 1, p. 20-26.

Palincsar, A.M.; Brown, A. 1984. Reciprocal Teaching of Comprehension Fostering and Comprehension Monitoring Activities. *Cognition and Instruction* (Hillsdale, NJ), Vol. 1, p. 117-76.

Paschal, R.; Weinstein, T.; Walberg. H.J. 1984. Effects of Homework: A Quantitative Synthesis. *Journal of Educational Research* (Washington DC), Vol. 78, p. 97-104.

Pearson, D. 1985. Reading Comprehension Instruction: Six Necessary Steps. *The Reading Teacher* (Newark, DE), Vol. 38, p. 724-38.

Peng, S.; Wright, D. 1994. Explanation of Academic Achievement of Asian American Students. *Journal of Educational Research* (Washington, DC), Vol. 87. No. 6, p. 346-52.

Stevenson. H.W.; Lee, S.Y.; Stigler, J.W. 1986. Mathematics Achievement of Chinese, Japanese, and American Children. *Child Development* (Chicago, IL), Vol. 56, p. 718-34.

Stigler, J.; Lee, S.; Stevenson, H. 1987. Mathematics Classrooms in Japan, Taiwan, and the United States. *Child Development* (Chicago, IL), Vol. 58, No. 1272-285.

Walberg, H.J. 1984. Improving the Productivity of America's Schools. *Educational Leadership* (Alexandria, VA), Vol. 41, No. 8, p. 19-27.

Walberg, H.J. 1986. Synthesis of Research on Teaching. *In:* Wittrock, M.C., ed. *Handbook of Research on Teaching*, New York, Macmillan.

Walberg, H.J. 1994. Homework. In: Husén, T.; Postlethwaite, T.N. eds. *International Encyclopaedia of Education*. 2nd ed. Oxford, UK, Pergamon.

Walberg, H.J.; Fredrick, W.C. 1991. *Extending Learning Time*. Washington, DC, U.S. Department of Education, Office of Educational Research and Improvement.

Walberg, H.J.; Haertel, G.D., eds. 1997. *Psychology and Educational Practice*. Berkeley, CA, McCutchan Publishing.

Walberg, H.J.; Paik, S.J. 1997. Home Environments for Learning. *In:* Walberg, H.J.; Haertel, G.D., eds. *Psychology and Educational Practice*, p. 356-68. Berkeley, CA, McCutchan Publishing.

Walker, C.H. 1987. Relative Importance of Domain Knowledge. *Cognition and Instruction* (Hillsdale, NJ), Vol. 4, No. 1, p. 25-42.

Wang, M.C. 1992. *Adaptive Education Strategies: Building on Diversity*. Baltimore, MD Paul H. Brookes Publishing.

Wang, M.C.; Haertel, G.D.; Walberg, H.J. 1993*a*. Toward a Knowledge Base for School Learning. *Review of Educational Research* (Washington, DC), Vol. 63, p. 249-94.

Wang, M.C.; Haertel. G.D.; Walberg, H.J. 1993*b*. What Helps Students Learn? *Educational Leadership* (Alexandria, VA), Vol. 51, No. 4, p. 74-79.

Wang, M.C.; Haertel, G.D.; Walberg, H.J. 1998. Models of Reform: A Comparative Guide. *Educational Leadership* (Alexandria, VA), Vol. 55, No. 7, p. 66-71.

Wang, M.C.; Oates, J.; Whiteshew, N. 1995. Effective School Responses to Student Diversity in Inner-City Schools: a Co-ordinated Approach. *Education and Urban Society* (Thousand Oaks, CA), Vol. 27, No. 4, p. 32-43.

Wang, M.C.; Zollers, N.J. 1990. Adaptive Education: An Alternative Service Delivery Approach. *Remedial and Special Education* (Austin, TX), Vol. 11, No. 1, p. 7-21.

Waxman, H.C.; Walberg, H.J. 1999. *New Directions for Teaching Practice and Research*, Berkeley, CA, McCutchan Publishing.

Weinert, F. 1989. The Relation Between Education and Development. *International Journal of Educational Research* (Tarrytown, NY), Vol. 13, No. 8, p. 827-948.

Wittrock, M.C., ed. 1986. *Handbook of Research on Teaching*. New York, Macmillan.

Courtesy: UNESCO's International Bureau of Education and Internation Academy of Education.

2

How Children Learn?

*Stella Vosniadou**

Introduction

The psychological principles described in this chapter summarize some of the important results of recent research on learning that is relevant for education. They attempt to integrate research coming from diverse areas of psychology, including educational, developmental, cognitive, social and clinical psychology. This research has offered us new insights into the learning process and the development of knowledge in many subject-matter areas. As a result, curricula and instruction are changing in schools today. They are attempting to become more student-centred than teacher-centred, to connect the school to real-life situations, and to focus on understanding and thinking rather than on memorization, drill and practice.

Although each principle is explained on its own, all twelve principles are best understood as an organised whole with one supporting the others. As a whole, these principles are meant to provide a comprehensive framework for the design of curricula and of instruction. Indeed, they are found behind a number of innovative programmes in schools across the world today.

* University of Athens, Greece.

We begin with a discussion of three principles that are widely recognized as forming the basis on which teachers should design the learning environments of today's schools; namely, learning environments that encourage students to be active learners, to collaborate with other students, and to use meaningful tasks and authentic materials. We continue with seven principles that focus on cognitive factors that are primarily internal, but also interact with environmental factors in important ways. Teachers need to take these principles into consideration in order to design more effective curricula and instruction. We end with a discussion of developmental and individual differences, and with motivational influences on learning. These last two areas are very important for learning and instruction, and—to be treated adequately—deserve to become independent booklets.

We have not dealt with a subject that is becoming very important in the schools of today—the use of information and communication technology to support learning. We have not done so because this area is too vast and we believe that a special booklet needs to be devoted to it.

In discussing each principle, we start by presenting a summary of the research findings and then continue describing the implications for teaching that follow from them. At the end, there is a list of references and suggested readings that provide further information on the principles that have been discussed.

Active Involvement

Learning requires the active, constructive involvement of the learner.

Research Findings

Learning at school requires students to pay attention, to observe, to memorize, to understand, to set goals and to assume responsibility for their own learning. These cognitive activities are not possible without the active involvement and engagement of the learner. Teachers must help students to become active and goal-oriented by building on their natural desire to explore, to understand new things and to master them.

In the Classroom

It is a challenge for teachers to create interesting and challenging learning environments that encourage the active involvement of students. The following are some suggestions as to how this can be done:

- Avoid situations where the students are passive listeners for long periods of time;
- Provide students with hands-on activities, such as experiments, observations, projects, etc;
- Encourage participation in classroom discussions and other collaborative activities;
- Organise school visits to museums and technological parks;
- Allow students to take some control over their own learning. Taking control over one's learning means allowing students to make some decisions about what to learn and how;
- Assist students in creating learning goals that are consistent with their interests and future aspirations.

Social Participation

Learning is primarily a social activity and participation in the social life of the school is central for learning to occur.

Research Findings

For many researchers, social participation is the main activity through which learning occurs. Social activity and participation begin early on. Parents interact with their children and through these interactions children acquire the behaviours that enable them to become effective members of society. According to the psychologist Lev Vygotsky, the way children learn is by internalizing the activities, habits, vocabulary and ideas of the members of the community in which they grow up.

The establishment of a fruitful collaborative and co-operative atmosphere is an essential part of school learning. Research has shown that social collaboration can boost student achievement, provided that the kinds of interactions that are encouraged contribute to learning. Finally, social activities are interesting in their own right and help to keep students involved in their academic work. Students work harder to improve the quality of their products (essays, projects, artwork, etc.) when they know that they will be shared with other students.

In the Classroom

Teachers can do many things to encourage social participation in ways that facilitate learning:

- They can assign students to work in groups and assume the role of a coach/co-ordinator who provides guidance and support to the groups;
- They can create a classroom environment that includes group workspaces where resources are shared;
- Through modelling and coaching, they can teach students how to co-operate with each other;
- They can create circumstances for students to interact with each other, to express their opinions and to evaluate other students' arguments;
- An important aspect of social learning is to link the school to the community at large. In this way, students' opportunities for social participation are enlarged.

Meaningful Activities

People learn best when they participate in activities that are perceived to be useful in real life and are culturally relevant.

Research Findings

Many school activities are not meaningful since students understand neither why they are doing them nor what their purpose and usefulness is. Sometimes school activities are not meaningful because they are not culturally appropriate. Many schools are communities where children from diverse cultures learn together. There are systematic cultural differences in practices, in habits, in social roles, etc., that influence learning. Sometimes meaningful activities for students coming from one cultural group are not meaningful to students who are coming from another cultural group.

In the Classroom

Teachers can make classroom activities more meaningful by situating them in an authentic context. An example of an authentic context is one in which the activity is typically used in real life. For example, students can improve their oral language and communication skills by participating in debates. They can improve their writing skills by being involved in the preparation of the classroom newspaper. Students can learn science by participating in a community or school environmental project. The school can be in contact with local scientists and invite them to lecture, or allow the students to visit their laboratories.

It is also important for teachers to be aware of the cultural differences of the children in their classroom and to respect these differences. They must see them as strengths to build on, rather than as defects. Children will feel differently in the classroom if their culture is reflected in the common activities. School routines that are unfamiliar to some children can be introduced gradually so that the transition can be less traumatic for ethnically diverse groups.

Relating New Information to Prior Knowledge

New knowledge is constructed on the basis of what is already understood and believed.

Research Findings

The idea that people's ability to learn something new follows from what they already know is not new, but more recent research findings have shown that the ability to relate new information to prior knowledge is critical for learning. It is not possible for someone to understand, remember or learn something that is completely unfamiliar. Some prior knowledge is necessary to understand the task at hand. But having the prerequisite prior knowledge is still not sufficient to ensure adequate results.

People must activate their prior knowledge in order to be able to use it for understanding and for learning. Research shows that students do not consistently see the relationships between new material that they read and what they already know. Research also shows that learning is enhanced when teachers pay close attention to the prior knowledge of the learner and use this knowledge as the starting point for instruction.

In the Classroom

Teachers can help students activate prior knowledge and use it for the task at hand. This can be done in a number of ways.

- Teachers can discuss the content of a lesson before starting in order to ensure that the students have the necessary prior knowledge and in order to activate this knowledge;
- Often students' prior knowledge is incomplete or there are false beliefs and critical misconceptions. Teachers do not simply need to know that students know something about the topic to be introduced. They need to investigate students' prior knowledge in detail so that false beliefs and misconceptions can be identified;
- Teachers may need to go back to cover important prerequisite material or ask the students to do some preparatory work on their own;
- Teachers can ask the kind of question that helps students see relationships between what they are reading and what they already know;
- Effective teachers can help students to grasp relationships and make connections. They can do so by providing a model or a scaffold that students can use as support in their efforts to improve their performance.

Being Strategic

People learn by employing effective and flexible strategies that help them to understand, reason, memorize and solve problems.

Research Findings

Children develop strategies to help themselves solve problems from an early age. For example, when pre-school children are told to go to the supermarket to buy a list of food items, they often repeat the items on their way to remember them better. These children have discovered rehearsal as a strategy to improve their memory without anybody telling them to do so. When they go to school, children need help from teachers to develop appropriate strategies for solving mathematics problems, when understanding texts, doing science, learning from other students, etc. Research shows that when teachers make systematic attempts to teach learning strategies to students substantial gains can result.

Strategies are important because they help students understand and solve problems in ways that are appropriate for the situation at hand. Strategies can improve learning and make it faster. Strategies may differ in their accuracy, in their difficulty of execution, in their processing demands and in the range of problems to which they apply. The broader the range of strategies that children can use appropriately, the more successful they can be in problem solving, in reading, in text comprehension and in memorizing.

In the Classroom

Teachers must recognize the importance of students knowing and using a variety of strategies. The teaching of strategies can be done directly or indirectly. In the later case, the teacher can give students a task and provide a model of the inquiry process or ask key questions. For example, in reading, teachers can explicitly show students how to outline the important points in a text and how to summarize them. Alternatively, they can ask a group of students to discuss a text and summarize it. They can help in this process by participating in the discussion and by asking critical questions. In science, teachers can show students how to conduct experiments; how to form hypotheses, how to keep a systematic record of their findings, and how to evaluate them.

It is important to ensure that students learn to use these strategies on their own and do not always rely on teachers to provide the necessary support. Teachers need to gradually fade their assistance and allow students to take greater responsibility for their learning.

Engaging in Self-Regulation and Being Reflective

Learners must know how to plan and monitor their learning, how to set their own learning goals and how to correct errors.

Research Findings

The term 'self-regulation' is used here to indicate students' ability to monitor their own learning, to understand when they are making errors, and to know how to correct them. Self-regulation is not the same as being strategic. People can sue strategies for learning mechanically without being fully aware of what they are doing. Self-regulation involves the development of specific strategies that help learners evaluate their learning, check their understanding and correct errors when appropriate.

Self-regulation requires reflection in the sense of being aware of one's own beliefs and strategies. Reflection can develop through discussion, debates and essays, where children are encouraged to express their opinions and defend them. Another important aspect of reflection is being able to distinguish appearance from reality, common beliefs from scientific knowledge, etc.

In the Classroom

Teachers can help students become self-regulated and reflective by providing opportunities:

- To plan how to solve problems, design experiments and read books;
- To evaluate the statements, arguments, solutions to problems of others, as well as of one's self;
- To check their thinking and ask themselves questions about their understanding—(Why am I doing what I am doing? How well am I doing? What remains to be done?);

- To develop realistic knowledge of themselves as learners—(I am good in reading, but need to work on my mathematics);
- To set their own learning goals;
- To know what are the most effective strategies to use and when to use them.

Restructuring Prior Knowledge

Sometimes prior knowledge can stand in the way of learning something new. Students must learn how to solve internal inconsistencies and restructure existing conceptions when necessary.

Research Findings

Sometimes existing knowledge can stand in the way of understanding new information. While this is often the case in the learning of science and mathematics, it can apply to all subject-matter areas. It happens because our current understanding of the physical and social world, of history, of theorizing about numbers, etc., is the product of thousands of years of cultural activity that has radically changed intuitive ways of explaining phenomena. For example, in the area of mathematics, many children make mistakes when they use fractions because they use rules that apply to natural numbers only. Similarly, in the physical sciences, students form various misconceptions. The idea that the Earth is round like a pancake or like a sphere flattened on the top happens because it reconciles the scientific information that the Earth is round, with the intuitive belief that it is flat and that people live upon its top. Such misconceptions do not apply only in young children. They are common in high school and college students as well.

In the Classroom

What can teachers do to facilitate the understanding of counter-intuitive information?

- Teachers need to be aware that students have prior beliefs and incomplete understandings that can conflict with what is being taught at school.

- It is important to create the circumstances where alternative beliefs and explanations can be externalized and expressed.
- Teachers need to build on the existing ideas of students and slowly lead them to more mature understandings. Ignoring prior beliefs can lead to the formation of misconceptions.
- Students must be provided with observations and experiments that have the potential of showing to them that some of their beliefs can be wrong. Examples from the history of science can be used for this purpose.
- Scientific explanations must be presented with clarity and, when possible, exemplified with models.
- Students must be given enough time to restructure their prior conceptions. In order to do this, it is better to design curricula that deal with fewer topics in greater depth than attempting to cover a great deal of topics in a superficial manner.

AIMING TOWARDS UNDERSTANDING RATHER THAN MEMORIZATION

Learning is better when material is organised around general principles and explanations, rather than when it is based on the memorization of isolated facts and procedures.

Research Findings

All teachers want their students to understand what they are learning and not to memorize facts in a superficial way. Research shows that when information is superficially memorized it is easily forgotten. On the contrary, when something is understood, it is not forgotten easily and it can be transferred to other situations (see also the next principle on transfer). In order to understand what they are being taught, students must be given the opportunity to think about what they are doing, to talk about it with other students and with teachers, to clarify it and to understand how it applies in many situations.

In the Classroom

How does one teach for understanding? The following are some tasks teachers can carry out in order to promote understanding of the material that has been taught:

- Ask students to explain a phenomenon or a concept in their own words;
- Show students how to provide examples that illustrate how a principle applies or how a law works;
- Students must be able to solve characteristic problems in the subject-matter area. Problems can increase in difficulty as students acquire greater expertise;
- When students understand the material, they can see similarities and differences, they can compare and contrast, and they can understand and generate analogies;
- Teach students how to abstract general principles from specific cases and generalize from specific examples.

HELPING STUDENTS LEARN TO TRANSFER

Learning becomes more meaningful when the lessons are applied to real-life situations.

Research Findings

Students often cannot apply what they have learned at school to solve real-world problems. For examples, they may learn about Newton's law at school but fail to see how they apply in real-life situations. Transfer is very important. Why should someone want to go to school if what is learned there does not transfer to other situations and cannot be used outside the school?

In the Classroom

Teachers can improve students' ability to transfer what they have learned at school by:

- Insisting on mastery of subject matter. Without an adequate degree of understanding, transfer cannot take place (see previous principle);

- Helping students see the transfer implications of the information they have learned;
- Applying what has been learned in one subject-matter area to other areas to which it may be related;
- Showing students how to abstract general principles from concrete examples;
- Helping students learn how to monitor their learning and how to seek and use feedback about their progress;
- Teach for understanding rather than for memorization (see previous principle).

TAKING TIME TO PRACTICE

Learning is a complex cognitive activity that cannot be rushed. It requires considerable time and periods of practice to start building expertise in an area.

Research Findings

Research shows that people must carry out a great deal of practice to acquire expertise in an area. Even small differences in the amount of time during which people are exposed to information can result in large differences in the information they have acquired. Cognitive psychologists Chase and Simon (1973) studied chess experts and found that they had often spent as many as 50,000 hours practising chess. A 35-year-old chess master who has spent 50,000 hours playing chess must have spent four to five hours on the chessboard from the age of 5 every day for thirty years! Less accomplished players have spent considerably less time playing chess.

Research shows that the reading and writing skills of high school students relate to the hours they have spent on reading and writing. Effective reading and writing requires a lot of practice. Students from disadvantaged environments who have less opportunities to learn and who miss school because of work or illness will not be expected to do as well at school compared to children who had more time to practice and acquire information.

In the Classroom

Many educational programmes are designed to increase one's exposure to learning situations preferably at an early age. Here are some recommendations for teachers that can help students spend more time on learning tasks:

- Increase the amount of time students spend on learning in the classroom;
- Give students learning tasks that are consistent with what they already know;
- Do not try to cover too many topics at once. Give students time to understand the new information;
- Help students engage in 'deliberate practice' that includes active thinking and monitoring of their own learning (see sections on self-regulation);
- Give students access to books so that they can practice reading at home.
- Be in contact with parents so that they can learn to provide richer educational experiences for their children.

DEVELOPMENTAL AND INDIVIDUAL DIFFERENCES

Children learn best when their individual differences are taken into consideration.

Research Findings

Research shows that there are major developmental differences in learning. As children develop, they form new ways of representing the world and they also change the processes and strategies they use to manipulate these representations. In addition, there are important individual differences in learning. Developmental psychologist Howard Gardner has argued that there are many dimensions of human intelligence other than the logical and linguistic skills that are usually valued in most school environments. Some children are gifted in music, others have exceptional spatial skills (required, for example, by architects and artists), or bodily/kinaesthetic abilities (required by athletes), or abilities to relate to other people, etc. Schools must create the best environment for the development of children taking into consideration such individual differences.

In the Classroom

The following are recommendations for creating the best environment for the development of children, while recognizing their individual differences:

- Learn how to assess children's knowledge, strategies and modes of learning adequately;
- Introduce children to a wide range of materials, activities and learning tasks that include language, mathematics, natural sciences, social sciences, art, music, movement, social understanding, etc;
- Identify students' areas of strength, paying particular attention to the interest, persistence and confidence they demonstrate in different kinds of activities;
- Support students' areas of strength and utilize these areas to improve overall academic performance;
- Guide and challenge students' thinking and learning;
- Ask children thought-provoking questions and give them problems to solve. Urge children to test hypotheses in a variety of ways;
- Create connections to the real world by introducing problems and materials drawn from everyday situations;
- Show children how they can use their unique profiles of intelligence to solve real-world problems;
- Create circumstances for students to interact with people in the community, and particularly with adults who are knowledgeable and enthusiastic about the kinds of things that are of interest to the students.

Creating Motivated Learners

Learning is critically influenced by learner motivation. Teachers can help students become more motivated learners by their behaviour and the statements they make.

Research Findings

Motivated learners are easy to recognize because they have a passion for achieving their goals and are ready to expand a great deal of effort. They also show considerable determination and persistence. This influences the amount and quality of what is learned. All teachers want to have motivated learners in their classrooms. How can they achieve this?

Psychologists distinguish between two kinds of motivation: extrinsic motivation and intrinsic motivation. Extrinsic motivation results when positive rewards are used to increase the frequency of a target behaviour. Praise, high grades, awards, money and food can be used for that effect. Intrinsic motivation is when learners actively participate in activities without having to be rewarded for it. The child who likes to put together puzzles for the fun of it is intrinsically motivated.

An important characteristic of intrinsically motivated learners is their belief that effort is important for success. Teachers can influence students' determination to achieve by their behaviour and the statements they make.

In the Classroom

Teachers must use encouraging statements that reflect an honest evaluation of learner performance:

- Recognize student accomplishments;
- Attribute student achievement to internal and not external factors (*e.g.* 'You have good ideas');
- Helps students believe in themselves (e.g. 'You are putting a lot of effort on maths and your grades have much improved');
- Provide feedback to children about the strategies they use and instruction as to how to improve them;
- Help learners set realistic goals.

It is also important to:

- Refrain from grouping students according to their ability. Ability grouping gives the message that ability is valued more than effort;
- Promote co-operation rather than competition. Research suggests that competitive arrangements that encourage students to work alone to achieve high grades and rewards tend to give the message that what is valued is ability and diminish intrinsic motivation;
- Provide novel and interesting tasks that challenge learners' curiosity and higher-order thinking skills at the appropriate level of difficulty.

REFERENCES

Bereiter, C. 1997. Situated Cognition and How to Overcome It. *In:* Kirshner, D.; Whitson, J.A.; eds. *Situated Cognition: Social, Semiotic, and Psychological Perspectives*, p. 281-300. Hillsdale, NJ, Erlbaum.

Boekaerts, M.; Pintrich, P.; Zeidner, M. 2000. *Handbook of Self-Regulation, New York, Academic Press.*

Bransford, J.D. 1979. *Human Cognition; Learning, Understanding and Remembering*. Belmont, CA, Wadsworth Publishing Co.

Bransford, T.D.; Brown, A.L.; Cocking, R.R., eds. 1999. *How People Learn: Brain, Mind, Experience and School*. Washington, DC, National Academy Press.

Brown, A.L. 1975. The Development of Memory; Knowing, Knowing About Knowing and Knowing How to Know. *In: Reese*, H.W., ed. *Advances in Child Development and Behaviour*, Vol. 10. New York, Academic Press.

Brown, A.L., et al., 1996. Distributed Expertise in the Classroom. *In:* Salomon, G., ed. *Distributed Cognitions: Psychological and Educational Considerations*. p. 188-228. Hillsdale, NJ, Erlbaum.

Brown, J.S.; Collins, A.; Duguid, P. 1989. Situated Cognition and the Culture of Learning. *Educational Researcher* (Washington, DC), Vol. 18, No. 1.

Bruer, J.T. 1993. *Schools for Thought*. Cambridge, MA, MIT Press.

Carretero M.; Voss, J., eds. 1994. *Cognitive and Instructional Processes in History and the Social Sciences*. Hillsdale, NJ, Erlbaum.

Case, R. 1978. Implications of Developmental Psychology for the Design of Effective Instruction. *In:* Lesgold, A.M., et. al., eds. *Cognitive Psychology and Instruction*, p. 441-63. New York, Plenum.

Chase, W. G.; Simon, H.A. 1973. The Mind's Eye in Chess. *In:* Chase, W.G. ed. *Visual Information Processing*. New York, Academic Press.

Chen, J., et. al. 1998. *Building on Children's Strengths: The Experience of Project Spectrum*. New York, Teachers College, Columbia University.

Coles, R. 1970. *Uprooted Children: The Early Life of Migrant Farm Workers*. New York, Harper and Row.

Collins, A.; Brown, J.S.; Newman, S.F. 1989. Cognitive Apprenticeship: Teaching the Craft of Reading, Writing and Mathematics. *In:* Resnick, L.B., ed. *Knowing, Learning and Instruction: Essays in Honor of Robert Glaser*, p. 453-84. Hillsdale, NJ, Lawrence Erlbaum.

Deci, E.L.; Ryan, R. 1985. *Intrinsic Motivation and Self-Determination in Human Behaviour*. New York, Plenum Press.

Driver, R; Guesne, E.: Tiberghien, A. eds. 1985. *Children's Ideas in Science*, Milton Keynes, United Kingdom, Open University Press.

Dweck, C.S. 1989. Motivation. *In:* Lesgold A.; Glaser, R. eds. *Foundations for a Psychology of Education*. p. 87-136. Hillsdale, NJ, Erlbaum.

Elmore, R.F.; Peterson, P.L.; McCarthy, S.J. 1996. *Restructuring in the Classroom: Teaching, Learning and School Organisation*. San Francisco, CA, Jossey-Bass.

Gardner, H. 1991. *The Unschooled Mind, How Children Think and How Schools Should Teach*. New York, Basic Books.

—. 1993. *Multiple Intelligences: The Theory in Practice*. New York. Basic Books.

Halpern, D.F., ed. 1992. *Enhancing Thinking Skills in the Sciences and Mathematics*. Hillsdale, NJ, Erlbaum.

Heath, S.B. 1983. *Ways With Words: Language, Life and Work in Communities and Classrooms*. Cambridge, United Kingdom, Cambridge University Press.

Lepper, M.; Hodell, M. 1989. Intrinsic Motivation in the Classroom. *In:* Ames, C.; Ames, R. eds. *Research on Motivation in Education*, Vol. 3, p. 73-105, New York, Academic Press.

Marton, F.; Booth, S. 1997. *Learning and Awareness*. Hillsdale, NJ, Erlbaum.

Mayer, R.E. 1987. *Educational Psychology: a Cognitive Approach*. Boston, MA, Little, Brown.

Palincsar, A.S.; Brown, A.L.; 1984. Reciprocal Teaching of Comprehension Monitoring Activities. *Cognition and Instruction* (Hillsdale, NJ), Vol. 1, p. 117-75.

Perkins, D. 1992. *Smart Schools: Better Thinking and Learning for Every Child*. Riverside, MJ, The Free Press.

Piaget, J. 1978. *Success and Understanding*. Cambridge, MA, Harvard University Press.

Resnick, L.B.; Klopfer, L.E., eds. 1989. *Toward the Thinking Curriculum: Current Cognitive Research*. Alexandria, VA, ASCD Books.

Rogoff, B. 1990. *Apprenticeships in Thinking: Cognitive Development in Social Context*. New York, Oxford University Press.

Scardamalia, M.; Bereiter, C. 1991. Higher Levels of Agency for Children in Knowledge Building: A Challenge for the Design of New Knowledge Media. *Journal of the Learning Sciences* (Hillsdale, NJ), No. 1, p. 37-68.

Schnotz, W.; Vosniadou, S.; Carretero, M. 1999. *New Perspectives on Conceptual Change*. Oxford, United Kingdom, Elsevier Science.

Spaulding, C.L. 1992. *Motivation in the Classroom*. New York, McGraw Hill.

Vosniadou, S.; Brewer, W.F. 1992. Mental Models of the Earth: A Study of Conceptual Change in Childhood. *Cognitive Psychology* San Diego, CA), No. 24, p. 535-58.

Vygotsky, L.S. 1978. *Mind in Society: The Development of Higher Psychological Processes*. Cambridge, MA, Harvard University Press.

White, B.Y.; Frederickson, J.R. 1998. Inquiry, Modelling and Metacognition: Making Science Accessible to All Students. *Cognition and Instruction* (Hillsdale, NJ), Vol. 16, No. 1, p. 13-117.

Courtesy: UNESCO's International Bureau of Education and International Academy of Education.

3

Teaching

*Jere Brophy**

Introduction

This chapter is a synthesis of principles of effective teaching that have emerged from research in classrooms. It addresses generic aspects of curriculum, instruction and assessment, as well as classroom organisation and management practices that support effective instruction. It focuses on learning outcomes but with recognition of the need for a supportive classroom climate and positive student attitudes towards schooling, teachers and classmates.

Much of the research support for these principles comes from studies of relationships between classroom processes (measured through observation systems) and student outcomes (most notably, gains in standardized achievement tests). However, some principles are rooted in the logic of instructional design (*e.g.* the need for alignment among a curriculum's goals, content, instructional methods and assessment measures). In addition, attention was paid to emergent theories of teaching and learning (*e.g.* socio-cultural, social, constructivist) and to the standards statements circulated by organisations representing the major school subjects. Priority was given to principles that have been

* Michigan State University, United States of America.

shown to the applicable under ordinary classroom conditions and associated with progress towards desired student outcomes.

The principles rest on a few fundamental assumptions about optimizing curriculum and instruction. First, school curricula subsume different types of learning that call for different types of teaching, and so no single teaching method (*e.g.* direct instruction, social construction of meaning) can be the method of choice for all occasions. An optimal programme will feature a mixture of instructional methods and learning activities.

Second, within any school subject or learning domain, students' instructional needs change as their expertise develops. Consequently, what constitutes an optimal mixture of instructional methods and learning activities will evolve as school years, instructional units and even individual lessons progress.

Third, students should learn at high levels of mastery yet progress through the curriculum steadily. This implies that, at any given time, curriculum content and learning activities need to be difficult enough to challenge students and extend their learning, but not so difficult as to leave many students confused or frustrated. Instruction should focus on the zone of proximal development, which is the range of knowledge and skills that students are not yet ready to acquire on their own but can acquire with help from their teachers.

A Supportive Classroom Climate

Students learn best within cohesive and caring learning communities

Research Findings

Productive contexts for learning feature an ethic of caring that pervades teacher/student and student/student interactions, and transcends gender, race, ethnicity, culture, socio-economic status, handicapping conditions and all other individual differences. Students are expected to manage instructional materials responsibly, participate thoughtfully in learning activities, and support the personal, social and academic well-being of all members of the classroom community.

In the Classroom

To create a climate for moulding their students into a cohesive and supportive learning community, teachers need to display personal attributes that will make them effective as models and socializers: a cheerful disposition, friendliness, emotional maturity, sincerity, and caring about students as individuals as well as learners. The teacher displays concern and affection for students, is attentive to their needs and emotions, and socializes them to display these same characteristics in their interactions with one another.

In creating classroom displays and in developing content during lessons, the teacher connects with and builds on the students' prior knowledge and experiences, including their home cultures. Extending the learning community from the school to the home, the teacher establishes and maintains collaborative relationships with parents and encourages their active involvement in their children's learning.

The teacher promotes a learning orientation by introducing activities with emphasis on what students will learn from them, treating mistakes as natural parts of the learning process, and encouraging students to work collaboratively and help one another. Students are taught to ask questions without embarrassment, to contribute to lessons without fear of their ideas being ridiculed, and to collaborate in pairs or small groups on many of their learning activities.

Opportunity to Learn

Students learn more when most of the available time is allocated to curriculum-related activities and the classroom management system emphasizes maintaining their engagement in those activities.

Research Findings

A major determinant of learning in any academic domain is the degree of exposure to the domain at school. The lengths of the school day and the school year create upper limits on students' opportunities to learn. Within these limits, the learning opportunities actually experienced by students depend on how much of the available time they spend participating in lessons and learning activities. Effective teachers allocate most of the available time to activities designed to accomplish instructional goals.

Research indicates that teachers who approach management as a process of establishing an effective learning environment tend to be more successful than teachers who emphasize their roles as disciplinarians. Effective teachers do not need to spend much time responding to behaviour problems because they use management techniques that elicit students' co-operation and sustain their engagement in activities. Working within the positive classroom climate implied by the principle of a learning community, the teacher articulates clear expectations concerning classroom behaviour in general and participation in lessons and learning activities in particular, teaches procedures that foster productive engagement during activities and smooth transitions between them, and follows through with any needed cues or reminders.

In the Classroom

There are more things worth learning than there is time available to teach them, and so it is essential that limited classroom time be used efficiently. Effective teachers allocate most of this time to lessons and learning activities rather than to non-academic pastimes that serve little or no curricular purpose. Their students spend many more hours each year on curriculum-related activities than do students of teachers who are less focused on instructional goals.

Effective teachers convey a sense of the purposefulness of schooling and the importance of getting the most out of the available time. They begin and end lessons on time, keep transitions short, and teach their students how to get started quickly and maintain focus when working on assignments. Good planning and preparation enable them to proceed through lessons smoothly without having to stop to consult a manual or locate an item needed for display or demonstration. Their activities and assignments feature stimulating variety and optimal challenge, which help students to sustain their task engagement and minimize disruptions due to boredom or distraction.

Successful teachers are clear and consistent in articulating their expectations. At the beginning of the year they model or provide direct instruction in desired procedures if necessary, and subsequently they cue or remind their students when these procedures are needed. They monitor the classroom continually, which enables them to respond to emerging problems before they become disruptive. When possible, they intervene in ways that do not disrupt lesson momentum or distract students who are working on assignments. They teach students strategies and procedures for carrying out recurring activities such as participating in whole-class lessons, engaging in productive discourse with classmates, making smooth transitions between activities, collaborating in pairs or small groups, storing and handling equipment and personal belongings, managing learning and completing assignments on time, and knowing when and how to get help. The teachers' emphasis is not on imposing situational control but on building students' capacity for managing their own learning, so that expectations are adjusted and cues, reminders and other managerial moves are faded out as the school year progresses.

These teachers do not merely maximize 'time on task', but spend a great deal of time actively instructing by elaborating content for students and helping them to interpret and respond to it. Their classrooms feature more time spent in interactive discourse and less time spent in solitary seatwork. Most of their instruction occurs during interactive discourse with students rather than during extended lecture presentations.

Note: The principle of maximizing opportunity to learn is not meant to imply maximizing the scope of the curriculum (*i.e.* emphasizing broad coverage at the expense of depth of development of powerful ideas). The breadth/depth dilemma must be addressed in curriculum planning. The point of the opportunity-to-learn principle is that, however the breadth/depth dilemma is addressed and whatever the resultant curriculum may be, students will make the most progress towards intended outcomes if most of the available classroom time is allocated to curriculum-related activities.

Note: Opportunity to learn is sometimes defined as the degree of overlap between what is taught and what is tested. This definition can be useful if both the curriculum content and the test content reflect the major goals of the instructional programme. Where this is not the case, achieving an optimal alignment may require making changes in the curriculum content or in the test content, or in both (see next principle).

CURRICULAR ALIGNMENT

All components of the curriculum are aligned to create a cohesive programme for accomplishing instructional purposes and goals.

Research Findings

Research indicates that educational policy-makers, textbook publishers and teachers often become so focused on content coverage or learning activities that they lose sight of the larger purposes and goals that are supposed to guide curriculum planning. Teachers typically plan by concentrating on the content they intend to cover and the steps involved in the activities their students will carry out, without giving much thought to the goals or intended outcomes of the instruction. Textbook publishers, in response to pressure from special interest groups, tend to keep expanding their content coverage. As a result, too many topics are covered in not enough depth; content exposition often lacks coherence and is cluttered with insertions; skills are taught separately from knowledge content rather than integrated with it; and in general, neither the students' texts nor the questions and activities suggested in the teachers' manuals are structured around powerful ideas connected to important goals.

Students taught using such textbooks may be asked to memorize parades of disconnected facts or to practise disconnected subskills in isolation instead of learning coherent networks of connected content structured around powerful ideas. These problems are often exacerbated by externally imposed assessment programmes that emphasize recognition of isolated bits of knowledge or performance of isolated subskills. Such problems can be minimized through goal-oriented curriculum development, in which curricular planning is guided by the overall purposes and goals of the instruction, not by miscellaneous content coverage pressures or test items.

In the Classroom

A curriculum is not an end in itself; it is a means of helping students to learn what is considered essential for preparing them to fulfil adult roles in society and realize their potential as individuals. Its goals are learner outcomes—the knowledge skills, attitudes, values are dispositions to action that society wishes to develop in its citizens. The goals are the reason for the existence of the curriculum, so that beliefs about what is needed to accomplish them should guide each step in curriculum planning and implementation. Goals are most likely to be attained if all of the curriculum's components (content clusters, instructional methods, learning activities and assessment tools) are selected because they are believed to be needed as means of helping students to accomplish the overall purposes and goals.

This involves planning curriculum and instruction to develop capabilities that students can use in their lives inside, and outside school, both now and in the future. In this regard, it is important to emphasize goals of understanding, appreciation and life application. Understanding means that students learn both the individual elements in a network of related content and the connections among them, so that they can explain the content in their own words and connect it to their prior knowledge. Appreciation means that students value what they are learning because they understand that there are good reasons for learning it. Life application means that students retain their learning in a form that makes it usable when needed in other contexts.

Content developed with these goals in mind is likely to be retained as meaningful learning that is internally coherent, well connected with other meaningful learning, and accessible for application. This is most likely to occur when the content itself is structured around powerful ideas and the development of this content through classroom lessons and learning activities focuses on these ideas and their connections.

Establishing Learning Orientations

Teachers can prepare students for learning by providing an initial structure to clarify intended outcomes and cue desired learning strategies.

Research Findings

Research indicates the value of establishing a learning orientation by beginning lessons and activities with advance organisers or previews. These introductions facilitate students' learning by communicating the nature and purpose of the activity, connecting it to prior knowledge and cueing the kinds of student responses that the activity requires. This helps students to remain goal-oriented and strategic as they process information and respond to the questions or tasks embodied in the activity. Good lesson orientations also stimulate students' motivation to learn by communicating enthusiasm for the learning or helping students to appreciate its value or application potential.

In the Classroom

Advance organisers orient students to what they will be learning before the instruction begins. They characterize the general nature of the activity and give students a structure within which to understand and connect the specifics that will be presented by the teacher or text. Such knowledge of the nature of the activity and the structure of its content helps students to focus on the main ideas and order their thoughts effectively. Therefore, before beginning any lesson or activity, the teacher should ensure that students know what they will be learning and why it is important for them to learn it.

Other way to help students learn with a sense of purpose and direction include calling attention to the activity's goals, overviewing main ideas or major steps to be elaborated, pretests that sensitize students to main points to learn, and pre-questions that stimulate their thinking about the topic.

Coherent Content

To facilitate meaningful learning and retention, content is explained clearly and developed with emphasis on its structure and connections.

Research Findings

Research indicates that networks of connected knowledge structured around powerful ideas can be learned with understanding and retained in forms that make them accessible for application. In contrast, disconnected bits of information are likely to be learned only through low-level processes such as rote memorizing, and most of these bits either are soon forgotten or are retained in ways that limit their accessibility. Similarly, skills are likely to be learned and used effectively if taught as strategies adapted to particular purposes and situations, with attention to when and how to apply them; but students may not be able to integrate and use skills that are learned only by rote and practised only in isolation from the rest of the curriculum.

In the Classroom

Whether in textbooks or in the teacher-led instruction, information is easier to learn to the extent that it is coherent—the sequence of ideas or events makes sense and the relationships among them are apparent. Content is most likely to be organised coherently when it is selected in a principled way, guided by ideas about what students should learn from studying the topic.

When making presentations, providing explanations or giving demonstrations, effective teachers project enthusiasm for the content and organise and sequence it so as to maximize its clarity and coherence. The teacher presents new information with reference to what students already know about the topic; proceeds in small steps sequenced in ways that are easy to follow; uses pacing, gestures and other oral communication skills to support comprehension; avoids vague or ambiguous language and digressions that disrupt continuity; elicits students' responses regularly to stimulate active learning and ensure that each step is mastered before moving to the next; finishes with a review of main points, stressing general integrative concepts; and follows up with questions or assignments that require students to encode the material in their own words and apply or extend it to new contexts. If necessary, the teacher also helps students to follow the structure and flow of the content by using outlines or graphic organisers that depict relationships, study guides that call attention to key ideas, or task organisers that help students keep track of the steps involved and the strategies they use to complete these steps.

In combination, the principles calling for curricular alignment and for coherent content imply that, to enable students to construct meaningful knowledge that they can access and use in their lives outside school, teachers need to: *(i)* retreat from breadth of coverage in order to allow time to develop the most important content in greater depth; *(ii)* represent this important content as networks of connected information structured around powerful ideas; *(iii)* develop the content with a focus on explaining these important ideas and the connections among them; and *(iv)* follow up with authentic learning activities and assessment measures that provide students with opportunities to develop and display learning that reflects the intended outcomes of the instruction.

Thoughtful Discourse

Questions are planned to engage students in sustained discourse structured around powerful ideas.

Research Findings

Besides presenting information and modelling application of skills, effective teachers structure a great deal of content-based discourse. They use questions to stimulate students to process and reflect on content, recognize relationships among and implications of its key ideas, think critically about it, and use it in problem solving, decision making or other higher-order applications. The discourse is not limited to rapidly paced recitation that elicits short answers to miscellaneous questions. Instead, it features sustained and thoughtful development of key ideas. Through participation in such discourse, students construct and communicate content-related understandings. In the process, they abandon naïve ideas or misconceptions and adopt the more sophisticated and valid embedded in the instructional goals.

In the Classroom

In the early stages of units when new content is introduced and developed, more time is spent in interactive lessons featuring teachers/student discourse than in independent work on assignments. The teacher plans sequences of questions designed to develop the content systematically and help students to construct understandings of it by relating it to their prior knowledge and collaborating in dialogue about it.

The forms and cognitive levels of these questions need to be suited to the instructional goals. Some primarily closed-end and factual questions might be appropriate when teachers are assessing prior knowledge or reviewing new learning, but accomplishing the most significant instructional goals requires open-ended questions that call for students to apply, analyse, synthesize or evaluate what they are learning. Some questions will admit of a range of possible correct answers, and some will invite discussion or debate (*e.g.* concerning the relative merits of alternative suggestions for solving problems).

Because questions are intended to engage students in cognitive processing and construction of knowledge, they should ordinarily be addressed to the class as a whole. This encourages all students, not just the one eventually called on, to listen carefully and respond thoughtfully to each question. After posing a question, the teacher needs to pause to allow students enough time to process it and at least begin to formulate responses, especially if the question is complicated or requires students to engage in higher-order thinking.

Thoughtful discourse features sustained examination of a small number of related topics, in which students are invited to develop explanations, make predictions, debate alternative approaches to problems, or otherwise consider the content's implications or applications. The teacher presses students to clarify or justify their assertions, rather than accepting them indiscriminately. In addition to providing feedback, the teacher encourages students to explain or elaborate on their answers or to comment on classmates' answers. Frequently, discourse that begins in a question-and-answer format evolves into an exchange of views in which students respond to one another as well as to the teacher and respond to statements as well as to questions.

Practice and Application Activities

Students need sufficient opportunities to practise and apply what they are learning, and to receive improvement-oriented feedback.

Research Findings

There are three main ways in which teachers help their students to learn. First, they present information, explain concepts and model skills. Second, they ask questions and lead their students in discussion and other forms of discourse surrounding the content. Third, they engage students in activities or assignments that provide them with opportunities to practise or apply what they are learning. Research indicates that skills practised to a peak of smoothness and automaticity tend to be retained indefinitely, whereas skills that are mastered only partially tend to deteriorate. Most skills included in school curricula are learned best when practice is distributed across time and embedded within a variety of tasks. Thus, it is important to follow up thorough initial teaching with occasional review activities and with opportunities for students to use what they are learning in a variety of application contexts.

In the Classroom

Practice is one of the most important yet least appreciated aspects of learning in classrooms. Little or no practice may be needed for similar behaviours such as pronouncing words, but practice becomes more important as learning becomes complex. Successful practice involves polishing skills that are already established at rudimentary levels in order to make them smoother, more efficient and more automatic, and not trying to establish such skills through trial and error.

Fill-in-the-blank worksheets, pages of mathematical computation problems and related tasks that engage students in memorizing facts or practising subskills in isolation from the rest of the curriculum should be minimized. Instead, most practice should be embedded within application contexts that feature conceptual understanding of knowledge and self-regulated application of skills. Thus, most practice of reading skills is embedded within lessons involving reading and interpreting extended text, most practice of writing skills is embedded within activities calling for authentic writing, and most practice of mathematics skills is embedded within problem-solving applications.

Opportunity to learn in school can be extended through homework assignments that are realistic in length and difficulty given the students' abilities to work independently. To ensure that students know what to do, the teacher can get them started on assignments in class, and then have them finish the work at home. An accountability system should be in place to ensure that students complete their homework assignments, and the work should be reviewed in class the next day.

To be useful, practice must involve opportunities not only to apply skills but also to receive timely feedback. Feedback should be informative rather than evaluative, helping students to assess their progress with respect to major goals and to understand and correct errors or misconceptions. At times when teachers are unable to circulate to monitor progress and provide feedback, they should arrange for students working on assignments to get feedback by consulting posted study guides or answer sheets or by asking peers designated to act as tutors or resource persons.

Scaffolding Students' Task Engagement

The teacher provides whatever assistance students need to enable them to engage in learning activities productively.

Research Findings

Research on learning tasks suggests that activities and assignments should be sufficiently varied and interesting to motivate student engagement, sufficiently new or challenging to constitute meaningful learning experiences rather than needless repetition, and yet sufficiently easy to allow students to achieve high rates of success if they invest reasonable time and effort. The effectiveness of assignments is enhanced when teachers first explain the work and go over practice examples with students before releasing them to work independently, and then circulate to monitor progress and provide help when needed. The principle of teaching within the students' zones of proximal development implies that students will need explanation, modelling, coaching and other forms of assistance from their teachers, but also that this teacher structuring and scaffolding will be faded as the students' expertise develops. Eventually, students should become able to use what they are learning autonomously and to regulate their own productive task engagement.

In the Classroom

Besides being well chosen, activities need to be effectively presented, monitored and followed up if they are to have their full impact. This means preparing students for an activity in advance, providing guidance and feedback during the activity, and leading the class in post-activity reflection afterwards. In introducing activities, teachers should stress their purposes in ways that will help students to engage in them with clear ideas about the goals to be accomplished. Then they might call students' attention to relevant background knowledge, model strategies for responding to the task or scaffold by providing information about task requirements. If reading is involved, for example, teachers might summarize the main ideas, remind students about strategies for developing and monitoring their comprehension as they read (paraphrasing, summarizing, taking notes, asking themselves questions to check understanding), distribute study guides that call attention to key ideas and structural elements, or provide task organizers that help students to keep track of the steps involved and the strategies that they are using.

One students begin working on activities or assignments, teachers should circulate to monitor their progress and provide assistance if necessary. Assuming that students have a general understanding of what to do and how to do it, these interventions can be kept brief and confined to minimal and indirect forms of help. If teacher assistance is too direct extensive, teachers will end up carrying out tasks for students instead of helping them learn to carry out the task themselves.

Teachers also need to assess performance for completion and accuracy. When performance is poor, they will need to provide re-teaching and follow-up assignments designed to ensure that content is understood and skills are mastered.

Most assignments will not have their full effects unless they are followed by reflection or debriefing activities in which the teacher reviews the task with the students, provides general feedback about performance, and reinforces main ideas as they relate to overall goals. Reflection activities should also include opportunities for students to ask follow-up questions, share task-related observations or experiences, compare opinions, or in other ways deepen their appreciation of what they have learned and how it relates to their lives outside school.

Strategy Teaching

The teacher models and instructs students in learning and self-regulation strategies.

Research Findings

General learning and study skills as well as domain-specific skills (such as constructing meaning from text, solving mathematical problems or reasoning scientifically) are most likely to be learned thoroughly and become accessible for application if they are taught as strategies to be brought to bear purposefully and implemented with metacognitive awareness and self-regulation. This requires comprehensive instruction that includes attention to propositional knowledge (what to do), procedural knowledge (how to do it) and conditional knowledge (when and why to do it). Strategy teaching is especially important for less able students who otherwise might not come to understand the value of consciously monitoring, self-regulating and reflecting upon their learning processes.

In the Classroom

Many students do not develop effective learning and problem-solving strategies on their own but can acquire them through modelling and explicit instruction from their teachers. Poor readers, for example, can be taught reading comprehension strategies such as keeping the purpose of an assignment in mind when reading; activating relevant background knowledge; identifying major points in attending to the outline and flow of content; monitoring understanding by generating and trying to answer questions about the content; or drawing and testing inferences by making interpretations, predictions and conclusions. Instruction should include not only demonstrations of and opportunities to apply the skill itself but also explanations of the purpose of the skill (what it does for the learner) and the occasions on which it would be used.

Strategy teaching is likely to be most effective when it includes cognitive modelling: the teacher thinks out loud while modelling use of the strategy. Cognitive modelling makes overt the otherwise covert thought processes that guide use of the strategy in a variety of contexts. It provides learners with first-person language ('self talk') that they can adapt directly when using the strategy themselves. This eliminates the need for translation that is created when instruction is presented in the impersonal third-person language of explanation or even the second-person language of coaching.

In addition to strategies used in particular domains or types of assignments, teachers can model and instruct their students in general study skills and learning strategies such as rehearsal (repeating material to remember it more effectively), elaboration (putting material into one's own words and relating it to prior knowledge), organisation (outlining material to highlight its structure and remember it), comprehension monitoring (keeping track of the strategies used to construct understanding and the degree of success achieved with them, and adjusting strategies accordingly), and affect monitoring (maintaining concentration and task focus, and minimizing performance anxiety and fear of failure).

When providing feedback as students work on assignments and when leading subsequent reflection activities, teachers can ask questions or make comments that help students to monitor and reflect on their learning. Such monitoring and reflection should focus not only on the content being learned, but also on the strategies that the students are using to process the content and solve problems. This will help the students to refine their strategies and regulate their learning more systematically.

Co-operative Learning

Students often benefit from working in pairs or small groups to construct understandings or help one another master skills.

Research Findings

Research indicates that there is often much to be gained by arranging for students to collaborate in pairs or small groups as they work on activities and assignments. Co-operative learning promotes affective and social benefits such as increased student interest in and valuing of subject matter, and increases in positive attitudes and social interactions among students who differ to gender, race, ethnicity, achievement levels and other characteristics.

Co-operative learning also create the potential for cognitive and metacognitive benefits by engaging students in discourse that requires them to make their task-related information-processing and problem-solving strategies explicit (and thus available for discussion and reflection. Students are likely to show improved achievement outcomes when they engage in certain forms of co-operative learning as an alternative to completing assignments on their own.

In the Classroom

Traditional approaches to instruction feature whole-class lessons followed by independent seatwork time during which students work alone (and usually silently) an assignments. Co-operative learning approaches retain the whole-class lessons but replace part of the individual seatwork time with opportunities for students to work together in pairs or small groups on follow-up practice and application activities. Co-operative learning can be used with activities ranging from drill and practice to learning facts and concepts, discussion and problem solving. It is perhaps most valuable as a way of engaging students in meaningful learning with authentic tasks in a social setting. Students have more chances to talk in pairs or small groups than in whole-class activities, and shy students are more likely to feel comfortable expressing ideas in these more intimate settings.

Some forms of co-operative learning call for students to help one another achieve individual learning goals, for example by discussing how to respond to assignments, checking work, or providing feedback or tutorial assistance. Other forms of co-operative learning call for students to work together to achieve a group goal by pooling their resources and sharing the work. For example, the group might conduct an experiment, assemble a college, or prepare a research report to be presented to the rest of the class. Co-operative learning models that call for students to work together to produce a group product often feature a division of labour among group participants (*e.g.* to prepare a biographical report, one group member will assume responsibility for studying the person's early life, another for the person's major accomplishments, another for the person's effects on society, and so on).

Co-operative learning methods are most likely to enhance learning outcomes if they combine group goals with individual accountability. This is, each group member will be held accountable for accomplishing the activity's learning goals (students know that any member of the group may be called on to answer any one of the group's questions or that they will all be tested individually on what they are learning).

Activities used in co-operative learning formats should be well suited to those formats. Some activities are most naturally carried out by individuals working alone, other by students working in pairs, and still others by small groups of three to six students.

Students should receive whatever instruction and scaffolding they may need to prepare them for productive engagement in co-operative learning activities. For example, teachers may need to show their students how to listen, share, integrate the ideas of others and handle disagreements constructively. During times when students are working in pairs or small groups, the teacher should circulate to monitor progress, make sure that groups are working productively and provide any assistance needed.

GOAL-ORIENTED ASSESSMENT

The teacher uses a variety of formal and informal assessment methods to monitor progress towards learning goals.

Research Findings

A well-developed curriculum includes strong and functional assessment components. These assessment components are aligned with the curriculum's goals, and so they are integrated with its content, instructional methods and learning activities, and designed to evaluate progress towards its major intended outcomes.

Comprehensive assessment does not just document students' ability to supply acceptable answers to questions of problems, it also examines the students' reasoning and problem-solving processes. Effective teachers routinely monitor their students' progress in this fashion, using both formal tests or performance evaluations and informal assessments of students' contributions to lessons and work on assignments.

In the Classroom

Effective teachers use assessment for evaluating students' progress in learning and for planning curriculum improvements, not just for generating grades. Good assessment includes data from many sources besides paper-and-pencil tests, and it addresses the full range of goals or intended outcomes (not only knowledge but also higher-order thinking skills and content-related values and dispositions). Standardized, norm-referenced tests might comprise part of the assessment programme (these tests are useful to the extent that they measure intended outcomes of the curriculum and attention is paid to students' performance on each individual item, not just total scores). However, standardized tests should ordinarily be supplemented with publisher-supplied curriculum-embedded tests (when these appear useful) and with teacher-made tests that focus on learning goals that are emphasized in instruction but not in external testing sources.

In addition, learning activities and sources of data other than tests should be used for assessment purposes. Everyday lessons and activities provide opportunities to monitor the progress of the class as a whole and of individual students, and tests can be augmented with performance evaluations such as laboratory tasks and observation checklists, portfolios of student papers or projects, and essays or other assignment that call for higher-order thinking and application. A broad view of assessment helps to ensure that the assessment component includes authentic activities that provide students with opportunities to synthesize and reflect on what they are learning, think critically and creatively about it, and apply it in problem-solving and decision-making contexts.

In general, assessment should be treated as an ongoing and integral part of each instructional unit. Results should be scrutinized to identify learner needs, misunderstandings or misconceptions that may need attention; to suggest potential adjustment in curriculum goals, instructional materials or teaching plans; and to detect weaknesses in the assessment practices themselves.

ACHIEVEMENT EXPECTATIONS

The teacher establishes and follows through on appropriate expectations for learning outcomes.

Research Findings

Research indicates that effective schools feature strong academic leadership that produces consensus on goal priorities and commitment to instructional excellence, as well as positive teacher attitudes towards students and expectations regarding their abilities to master the curriculum. Teacher effects research indicates that teachers who elicit strong achievement gains accept responsibility for doing so. They believe that their students are capable of learning and that they (the teachers) and capable of and responsible for teaching them successfully. If students do not learn something the first time, they teach it again, and if the regular curriculum materials do not do the job, they find or develop others that will.

In the Classroom

Teachers' expectations concerning what their students are capable of accomplishing (with teacher help) tend to shape both what teachers attempt to elicit from their students and what the students come to expect from themselves. Thus, teachers should form and project expectations that are as positive as they can be while still remaining realistic. Such expectations should represent genuine beliefs about what can be achieved and therefore should be taken seriously as goals towards which to work in instructing students.

It is helpful if teachers set goals for the class and for individuals in terms of floors (minimally acceptable standards), not ceilings. Then they can let group progress rates, rather than limits adopted arbitrarily in advance, determine how far the class can go within the time available. They can keep their expectations for individual students current by monitoring their progress closely and by stressing current performance over past history.

At the very least, teachers should expect all their students to progress sufficiently to enable them to perform satisfactorily at the next level. This implies holding all students accountable for participating in lessons and learning activities and for turning in careful and completed work on assignments. It also implies that, in addition to the other elements of good teaching summarized in the preceding principles, struggling students will receive whatever extra time, instruction and encouragement are needed to enable them to meet expectations.

When individualizing instruction and giving students feedback, teachers should emphasize continuous progress relative to previous levels of mastery rather than how students compare with their classmates or with standardized test norms. Instead of merely evaluating relative levels of success, teachers can diagnose learning difficulties and provide feedback accordingly. If students have not understood an explanation or demonstration, teachers can follow through by re-teaching (if necessary, in a difficult way rather than by merely repeating the original instruction).

In general, teachers are likely to be most successful when they think in terms of stretching students' minds by stimulating them are encouraging them to achieve as much as they can, not in terms of 'protecting' them from failure or embarrassment.

Conclusion

To date, most research on teaching has been conducted in the United States, Canada, Western Europe and Australia, and so the degree to which findings apply to other countries has yet to be addressed. The principles presented in this booklet are believed to apply universally, however, for two reasons. First, research done all over the world suggests that schooling is much more similar than different across countries and cultures. The day is divided into periods used for teaching each of the subjects included in the curriculum, and teaching includes whole-class lessons in which content is developed through teachers explanation and teacher/student interaction, followed by practice and application activities that students work on individually or in pairs or small groups. Second, the principles refer to generic aspects of teaching that cut across grade-levels and school subjects, not to particular curriculum content. In summary, these principles ought to apply universally because they focus on basic and universal aspects of formal schooling. They still require adaptation to the local context, however, including relevant characteristics of the nation's school system and the students' cultures.

The genetic principles featured in this booklet need to be supplemented with more specific principles that apply to the teaching of particular school subjects to particular types of students. Readers interested in planning instruction for particular grade levels and subject areas can consult the scholarly literature in the subject areas for elaborations on and additions to the principles outlined here.

Finally, although twelve principles are highlighted for emphasis and discussed individually, each principle should be applied in conjunction with the others. That is, the principles are meant to be understood as mutually supportive components of a coherent approach to teaching in which the teacher's plans and expectations, the classroom learning environment and management system, the curriculum content and instructional materials, and the learning activities and assessment methods are all aligned as means of helping students attain intended outcomes.

REFERENCES

Ausubel, D. 1968. *Educational Psychology: A Cognitive View*. New York, Holt, Rinehart and Winston.

Beck, I.; McKeown, M. 1988. Toward Meaningful Accounts in History Texts for Young Learners. *Educational Researcher* (Washington, DC), Vol. 17, N°, 6, p. 31-39.

Bennett, N.; Dunne, E. 1992. *Managing Small Groups*. New York, Simon and Schuster.

Brophy, J. 1983. Classroom Organisation and Management. *The Elementary School Journal* (Chicago, Il), Vol. 83, p. 265-85.

———, 1998. *Motivating Students to Learn*, Boston, McGraw-Hill.

Brophy, J.; Alleman, J. 1991. Activities as Instructional Tools: A Framework for Analysis and Evaluation. *Educational Researcher* (Washington, DC), Vol. 20, N°. 4, p. 9-23.

Clark, C.; Peterson, P. 1986. Teachers' Thought Processes. *In:* Wittrock, M.C., ed. *Handbook of Research on Teaching*, 3rd ed., p. 225-296, New York, Macmillan.

Cooper, H. 1994. *The Battle Over Homework: An Administrator's Guide to Setting Sound and Effective Policies*. Thousand Oaks, CA, Corwin.

Creemers, B.; Scheerens, J., Guest eds. 1989. Developments in School Effectiveness Research. *International Journal of Educational Research* (Oxford, UK), Vol. 13, p. 685-825.

Dempster, F. 1991. Synthesis of Research on Reviews and Tests. *Educational Leadership* (Alexandria, VA), Vol. 48, N°. 7, p. 71-76.

Denham, C.; Lieberman, A., eds. 1980. *Time to Learn*. Washington, DC, National Institute of Education.

Doyle, W. 1986. Classroom Organisation and Management. *In:* Wittrock, M.C., ed. *Handbook of Research on Teaching*, 3rd ed., p. 392-431. New York, Macmillan.

Good, T.; Brophy, J. 1986. School Effects. *In:* Wittrock, M.C., ed. *Handbook of Research on Teaching*, 3rd ed., p. 570-602. New York, Macmillan.

———, 2000. *Looking in Classrooms*, 8th ed. New York, Longman.

Jhonson, D.; Jhonson, R. 1994. *Learning Together and Alone: Cooperative, Competitive, and Individualistic Learning*, 4th ed. Boston, Allyn & Bacon.

Knapp, M. 1995. *Teaching for Meaning in High-Poverty Classrooms*. New York, Teachers College Press.

Meichenbaum, D.; Biemiller, A. 1998. *Nurturing Independent Learners: Helping Students Take Charge of Their Learning*. Cambridge, MA, Brookline.

Newmann, F. 1990. Qualities of Thoughtful Social Studies Classes: An Empirical Profile. *Journal of Curriculum Studies* (Basingstoke, UK), Vol. 22, p. 253-275.

Pressley, M.; Beard El-Dinary, P. Guest eds. 1993. Special Issue on Strategies Instruction. *The Elementary School Journal* (Chicago, IL), Vol. 94, p. 105-284.

Rosenshine, B. 1968. To explain: A Review of Research. *Educational Leadership* (Alexandria, VA) N°. 26, p. 275-280.

Rosenshine, B.; Meister, C. 1992. The use of Scaffolds for Teaching Higher-level Cognitive Strategies. *Educational Leadership* (Alexandria, VA), Vol. 49, N°. 7, p. 26-33.

Rowe, M. 1986. Wait time: Slowing Down May be a Way of Speeding Up! *Journal of Teacher Education* (Thousand Oaks, CA), Vol. 37, p. 43-50.

Sergiovanni, T. 1994. *Building Community in Schools*. San Francisco, Jossey-Bass.

Shuell, T. 1996. Teaching and Learning in a Classroom Context. *In:* Berliner, D.; Calfee, R. eds. *Handbook of Educational Psychology*, p. 726-764. New York, Macmillan.

Slavin, R. 1990. *Cooperative Learning: Theory, Research, and Practice*. Englewood Cliffs, NJ, Prentice-Hall.

Stiggins, R. 1997. *Student-Centered Classroom Assessment*, 2nd ed. Upper Saddle River, NJ, Prentice-Hall.

Teddlie, C.; Stringfield, S. 1993. *Schools Make a Difference: Lessons Learned From a 10-Year Study of School Effects*. New York, Teachers College Press.

Tharp, R.; Gallimore, R. 1988. *Rousing Minds to Life: Teaching, Learning, and Schooling in Social Context*. Cambridge, Cambridge University Press.

Wang, M.; Haertel, G.; Walberg, H. 1993. Toward a Knowledge base for School Learning. *Review of Educational Research* (Washington, DC) Vol. 63, p. 249-294.

Weinstein, C.; Mayer, R. 1986. The Teaching of Learning Strategies. *In:* Wittrock, M.C., ed. *Handbook of Research on Teaching*, 3rd ed., p. 315-27. New York, Macmillan.

Wiggins, G. 1993. *Assessing Student Performance: Exploring the Purpose and Limits of Testing*. San Francisco, Jossey-Bass.

Courtesy: UNESCO's International Bureau of Education and International Academy of Education.

Tutoring

*Keith Topping**

Introduction

Tutoring can be defined as people who are not professional teachers helping and supporting the learning of others in an interactive, purposeful and systematic way. It is most usually done on a one-to-one basis, in a pair.

Tutors can be parents or other adult carers, brothers and sisters, other members of the family, other learners from the peer group, and various kinds of volunteers. Children as young as 5-years-old have learned to tutor effectively. Everyone can be a tutor—everybody can help somebody with something. In helping others to learn, tutors often learn themselves.

Tutoring is a very old practice. It was common in Ancient Greece and Rome, and is recorded in ancient texts even before then. Over the centuries it has gone up and down in popularity, but it has never gone away.

Tutors do not need to be 'experts' in the content or skill they are tutoring. But it is usually best if they know a bit more than their tutees. (The word 'tutee' will be used in this chapter for

* University of Dundee, Scotland.

the learner who is tutored). However, if tutors are much more advanced than the tutees, they are likely to become bored with the content the tutee has to learn, and will not gain much themselves.

Tutoring does not necessarily need any special materials. Tutors should not try to imitate what they think a professional teacher might do, because they do not have enough background knowledge for that.

Tutors should not just support, prompt or 'scaffold' the tutee towards the 'right' answer. They should also challenge and extend the tutee's fixed ideas. May be there is more than one 'right' answer.

Tutoring might be effective in different ways for different pairs. Compared to professional teaching, it can give:

- more practice;
- more activity and variety;
- more individualized help;
- more questioning;
- simpler vocabulary;
- more modelling and demonstration;
- more local relevant examples;
- higher disclosure of misunderstanding;
- more prompting and self-correction;
- more immediate feedback and praise;
- more opportunities for generalization;
- more insight into learning (metacognition); and
- more self-regulation and ownership of the learning process.

Both tutees and tutors can also: learn to give and receive praise, develop social skills and wider contacts, develop communication skills (listening, explaining, questioning, summarizing), and develop greater self-esteem.

Simplistic forms of tutoring, focussing on drill and practice, do not exploit the full potential of tutoring. However, tutoring has its dangers.

While a tutor can offer a greater *quality* of individual support than a professional teacher can, the *quality* of that support is likely to be significantly poorer than that of a professional teacher. The detection of errors and misconceptions by tutors might be much less reliable than that by a teacher. Tutors might tell or show their tutees something which is actually incorrect, *i.e.* reinforce mistakes. Tutors might become impatient and just tell their tutee the right answer, or do the task for them, in which case the tutee will learn very little.

Tutoring can be done to help with work from school or college, or with any kind of learning work from anywhere. However, the tutor might not be sure exactly how the school wants to work to be done—especially if it has been a long time since the tutor was at school. Remember tutors are not expected to know everything. They should always be ready to say 'I am not sure' or 'this is my way, but it is not the only way'.

Despite these potential difficulties, a great deal of research evidence shows that tutoring can be very effective—and a very cost-effective way of raising achievement (Bloom, 1984; Cohen, Kulik and Kulik, 1982; Devin-Sheehan, Feldman and Allen, 1976; Levine, Glass and Meister, 1987; Rohrbeck et al.; 1999; Sharpley and Sharpley, 1981; Topping and Ehly, 1998; Walberg and Haertel, 1997).

Nevertheless, given the potential weaknesses as well as strengths of tutoring outlined here, it is important that tutoring is well structured and of good quality. Effectiveness reported in the research literature will not ensure effectiveness right there where you are. The quality of implementation is crucial. Tutors should be clear about how they can help, and how not.

Ten research-based 'Principles' for effective tutoring are given and discussed in this chapter. The principles are of three types:

- General principles of how to tutor—for tutors;
- Principles of how to tutor reading, writing and mathematics—for tutors; and
- Principles of how to organise tutoring—for teachers and organisers of tutoring.

References and suggestions for further reading are found at the end of the chapter.

Real-Life Goals

Agree a consistent time, target tutee's real-life goals, and balance support and challenge.

Research Findings

Time-on-task is a major factor in effective learning. Learning in frequent short sessions is more effective than in occasional long sessions.

The tutees' motivation will be highest for their own real-life goals. However, these might be short-term and focused only on task completion, and need broadening.

Tutoring should start at the tutee's current point of understanding. Tutors must establish where this is, and uncover relevant misconceptions. Tutoring must then proceed in small steps from this point.

Learning strategies is more important than memorizing subject content. Schoolteachers do not have enough time to talk with individual learners about their strategies, or explore deep understanding. This is where tutoring can be especially helpful (Gage and Berliner, 1998; Topping and Ehly, 1998).

Practical Applications

- ***Consistent and Regular Time:*** Tutor and tutee must agree how much time they can give to working together. How often will you meet each week? How long is each session? Over how many weeks? Where? Do not start anything you cannot keep up or finish. Regular meetings are needed to build up a trusting and comfortable tutoring relationship.

- ***Target Tutee's Real-life Goals*.** Tutees often have strong ideas on what they need help with. However, these ideas can be very short-term. Tutees might think more of getting their written homework done 'correctly' (so their teacher is not angry with them), than of really understanding the subject. Tutors have to start with the tutee's immediate concerns. But tutors should talk with tutees about their goals, encouraging them to consider wider and deeper understanding. Of course, this does not mean that tutors make tutees learn what the tutor is interested or expert in, or to think just like the tutor.

- ***Explore Understanding:*** Tutors need to find out what tutees already know—and what they think they know that is actually incorrect. Talking to explore deep understanding is the way to do this. Explore varied examples to make sure tutees can really use what they know in different contexts.

- ***Small Steps:*** Tutees often need to learn in very small steps. Do not expect them to make big leaps. Tutors often forget how long it took them to really understand something themselves.

- ***Balance Support and Challenge:*** Tutoring is intended to be supportive—to help the tutee in their struggle to understand. But totors should not just give tutees the right answer, or just tell or show them how to do something. This might feel helpful, but it will only result in mechanical learning without real understanding—remembering *what*. Understanding the process of *how* to find the right answer is the most important thing. So tutoring should be more than repeated drill and practice. Sometimes tutors will find that tutees have fixed ideas that are too narrow or just wrong. Then the tutor must challenge the tutee (in a gentle and helpful way), to help them loosen and then reorganise and improve the quality of their thinking.

Question and Prompt

Question, pause for thinking time and then prompt.

Research Findings

Talking at people for a long time is not an effective way of helping them to learn. The time you have allocated to tutoring must be spent tutoring if it is to have an effect. A variety of tasks and ways of responding to tasks helps prevent tutees and tutors from losing interest. Different kinds of questioning have very different effects on learners. Tutees must be allowed time to understand questions or tasks, relate them to their previous experience, and devise a relevant strategy. Prompting should be graduated, minimal for the required effect and various in type.

Practical Applications

- ***Avoid Lectures:*** Do not give tutees long, complicated explanations. Keep everything short, to the point and in simple words. Give positive instructions for what to do. Do not emphasize what *NOT* to do. If necessary, explain again briefly, but in different words.
- ***Review:*** Often it is helpful to briefly review what you learned in your previous tutoring session.
- ***Concentrate:*** Stay focused on the task in hand. Do not drift off into irrelevant conversation. Tutoring time is precious. Use it well. But have some fun while learning.
- ***Variety:*** Mix up: easy and hard tasks; short and long; highly structured and open-ended; talking, reading and writing.
- ***Question:*** Do not just ask for a fact or one-word answer. Ask questions that are open-ended and encourage the tutee to talk. But do not make them too complicated. Ask questions that will make the tutee think and reveal their understanding (or misunderstanding). Ask questions that make the tutee apply, analyse, predict, classify, synthesize, justify or

evaluate what they are learning. Some of these questions will have more than one 'right answers. Do not accept guesses.

- *Thinking Time:* Do not expect the tutee to respond to a question immediately. They will need some thinking time. Tutors can give them that, while school teachers often cannot.

- *Prompt:* Do not just tell the tutee the answer. Give them a small clue about how to work out the right answer. This might be a drawing or a gesture (for example), as well as more spoken words. Give just enough support to enable to tutee to be successful with some effort—no more.

CHECK AND CORRECT ERRORS

Observe performance; check for errors; ensure all errors are corrected.

Research Findings

Errors are a positive learning opportunity if recognized as errors. But if not recognized, errors compound faulty learning. Tutors have more time than school teachers to observe carefully for errors. But they might not be so good at actually recognizing them.

Tutors also have more time than teachers to intervene in a way that encourages self-correction. Self-correction is widely recognized as an important step towards developing metacognition (understanding *how* you learn) and self-managed learning.

Tutors are much less likely than teachers to be 'experts' in the subject. Accordingly, tutors benefit from access to some 'master' version of correctness or a perfect model. Otherwise they might reinforce errors (Topping and Ehly, 1998).

Practical Applications

- *Observe Tutee Performance Closely:* If errors are not seen and corrected, much faulty learning will take place.

Some errors might be just carelessness. But many will show a failure to understand.

- *Check for Errors:* When you see an error, try to intervene positively. Avoid just saying 'no!' First, suggest to your tutee that you think they might have made an error. Encourage them to find where. If they cannot find where, given them a clue to help them locate the error.
- *Promote Self-correction:* When they have found it, talk about the nature of the error. In what way is it wrong? Why? How can it be put right? Through this discussion, you give the tutee the chance to put the error right themselves (self-correct). This is much better for their learning and for their confidence.
- *Correction Procedure:* Of course, if they try to self-correct but still do not get it right, you will need to intervene more. If all else fails, you might need to: demonstrate or model the correct response; lead to prompt the tutee to imitate this; check that the tutee can produce the correct response without help.
- *Ensure Correct Correction:* Tutors do not know everything. So there is a risk they will not notice all the errors the tutee makes. Even worse, they might insist some answers are wrong, when actually they are correct. Or they might see the tutee has got something wrong, but get it wrong themselves in trying to correct it. In those kinds of tutoring where there are 'right answers' (for example, mathematics problems), it is helpful if the tutor has some master source of reference (like the correct answers on a separate sheet or in the back of the book). This might be especially necessary if tutor and tutee are not very different in ability in the subject.

Discuss and Praise

Discuss, praise and summarize/review.

Research Findings

Discussion leads tutees to actively process information and develops deeper understanding, rather than just learning facts by rote.

Praise is a powerful form of feedback, especially if it comes from someone with whom the tutee has a good relationship. Research has clarified ways to make praise especially effective.

A summarizing discussion should come at the end of the tutoring session. Reviewing the most important things that have been learned will help the tutee remember. This review discussion also leads naturally into planning what you might do in the next session. (Brophy, 1981; Good and Brophy, 1995; Topping and Ehly, 1998).

Practical Applications

- ***Discuss:*** The questioning mentioned in Chapter 2 and the promotion of self-correction mentioned in Chapter 3 should lead into elaborated discussions. These will help to establish deeper and wider understanding in the tutee—and perhaps also in the tutor!
- ***Praise:*** Most tutors do not praise their tutees as much as they think they do. Most tutors also criticize their tutees more than they think they do. Try to observe your own tutoring behaviour carefully. Tutoring is a private situation that should be within a context of trust. Embarrassment about giving and receiving praise publicly should not be a problem. So give more praise!
- ***When to Praise:*** Praise for success with particularly hard problems or tasks. Praise for self-correction. Praise for increasing time-span without error. Praise for effort as well as success when the tutee is struggling. Praise 'better efforts' even if still not quite right. Praise increasing tutee independence. At the end of the session, give praise for the whole session. Write some praise on any record of the session.
- ***Effective Praise:*** Praise specifying the reason for it—say exactly what the tutee has done well. Vary the praise—use as many different praise words as you can think of. See if your tutee can think of some more! Praise as if you mean it—sound and look pleased! Smile, at least.

- ***Summarize/Review:*** At strategic points during the tutoring session, and certainly at the end of it, ask the tutee to summarize or review the key or main points that have been learned. You might be surprised at what they think are the main points. You might need to remind them of one or two important things, which they already seem to have forgotten. Have a final discussion and agree about the main points. Do not try to cram in too many 'main' points. This is all good preparation for the review or recapitulation that should start your next session.

READING: SUPPORT AND REVIEW

Support the tutee through challenging text and discuss and review to ensure understanding.

Research Findings

There is no doubt that tutoring in reading can be effective (Cohen, Kulik and Kulik, 1982; Fuchs and Fuchs, 1998; Wasik and Slavin, 1993). However, structured methods tend to be most effective.

To advice given here is based on the model of Duolog Reading, a specific structure form of paired reading. This is one of the most extensively researched of educational interventions. There are several major reviews of the many studies in the research literature (Topping, 1995, 2001; Topping and Lindsay, 1992; Topping and Whiteley, 1990). Review of multiple unselected project evaluations in one large school district will also be found here. This gives a more realistic indication of real-world effectiveness, which is still impressive. Most of these studies are outcome studies, measuring improved reading skills in a variety of ways. A substantial number involved control or comparison groups. There is also evidence of enduring gains at follow-up (Topping, 1992). Studies show that the method tends to result in: fewer refusals (greater confidence); greater fluency; greater use of the context; greater likelihood of self-correction; fewer errors (greater accuracy); and better phonic skills.

In the recent review of the effectiveness of twenty interventions in reading (Brooks et al., 1998), Duolog reading ranked as one of the most effective. One or two other methods produced more spectacular results, but only with very small numbers of children. By contrast, Duolog reading has been demonstrated to be effective with thousands of children in hundreds of schools in many countries. Tutors and tutees can be trained in the method in a short space of time. It can be used with any reading material available, and so is very flexible and cost-effective.

Practical Applications

- ***Select Material:*** Have the tutee chose any reading material of high interest to them. Difficulty should be above the tutee's independent readability level, but not above the tutor's.
- ***Read Together*:** Support the tutee by both reading all the words aloud together. Adapt your reading speed to exactly match that of the tutee. The tutee must read every word.
- ***Correct Errors:*** When the tutee reads a word wrong, just tell the tutee the correct way to say the word. (Do not give clues, or the flow of reading will be interrupted.) The tutee must repeat it correctly. Then you continue. Always correct all errors this way, and no other way.
- ***Pause:*** However, do not jump in and put the word right straight away. Pause and give the tutee four seconds. If they put it right by themselves (self-correct) in this time, there is no need to interfere. (However, with a reader who rushes, you might need to pause for less time, and finger point back to the error word).
- ***Agree on a Signal for Reading Alone:*** Agree on a way for the tutee to signal to stop 'reading together', for when the tutee wants to read an easier section without support. This signal could be a knock, a sign or a hand squeeze. The tutor must stop 'reading together' immediately at the signal.

- ***Return to Reading Together:*** Sooner or later while 'reading alone' the tutee will make an error, which they cannot self-correct within four seconds. Correct the error (as above) *and* join back in 'reading together'.
- ***Continue:*** Go on like this, switching from 'reading together' to 'reading alone', to give the tutee just as much help as they need at any moment, but no more. 'Reading together' will still be needed as the tutee moves on to harder and harder books.
- ***Praise:*** Praise your tutee for: good reading of hard words; signalling for 'reading alone'; reading alone correctly for longer; getting all the words in a sentence right; and self-correcting. Try to use a variety of different praise words, and *look* pleased.
- ***Review:*** Talk about the book. Why it is interesting? Talk about the meaning of difficult words. What were the main ideas in the book? In what order?

WRITING: MAP AND EDIT

Help generate and map ideas; help scribe and edit rough drafts.

Research Findings

Peer assessment of writing is increasingly common in schools (O'Donnell and Topping, 1998). There are many descriptive reports of various kinds of 'collaborative writing', but few rigorous outcome studies involving school-age tutees. In Daiute's (1989) study of 9-12 year-old writing partners, it was clear they needed to be both planful (organised and controlled) and playful (exploring ideas and words). Daiute (1990) found boys successfully balanced play and control strategies, while girls tended to over-rely on control. Daiute and Dalton (1993) compared individual and collaborative writing in low-achieving 7-9 year-old children. They found both same-ability and cross-ability collaborative pairing had benefits.

The advice given here is based upon the 'paired writing' model (Topping, 1995, 2001). This includes in a systematic way many elements widely accepted as good practice. Three major controlled studies of this method have been reported. One project involved 11 year-old tutors working with 5-year-old emergent writers (Nixon and Topping, in press). The tutees improved significantly more than comparison children did. Another project involved same age tutoring with 8-year-olds (comparing fixed-role cross-ability and reciprocal-role same-ability tutoring) (Sutherland and Topping, 1999). Both tutors and tutees in both groups showed significant subsequent improvement in individual writing. However, the gains for tutors in the cross-ability group did not appear immediately. The third project involved same-age cross-ability tutoring with 10-year-olds (Yarrow and Topping, in press). Again, 'paired writers' showed significantly greater gains than children who wrote alone, whether tutors or tutees.

Practical Applications

- *Generate Ideas:* Talk about the purpose and audience for the writing. Talk about the tutee's ideas. Stimulate ideas by asking questions (such as Who? Do? What? To? With? Where? When? How? Why?— in any relevant order). Make brief one-word notes on the tutee's ideas.
- *Map Ideas:* Review the ideas. Have the tutee number the ideas in the best order. Or divide them into sections, and put the sections in order. Draw lines linking related ideas, making an 'ideas map'. Use colours or underlining if it helps. This map forms a plan for the next step.
- *Draft:* From the map, begin to write a rough version of the text. The tutee should say what they want to communicate, while, the tutor does as much of the actual writing down as the tutee needs. The tutor may: do all the writing; only write in the hard words; show the tutee how to write the hard words for the tutee to copy in; or only tell the tutee how to spell hard words. Do not worry about spelling, punctuation or grammar at this stage.

- ***Read:*** The tutor reads the draft aloud, with as much expression and attention to punctuation as possible. Then the tutee does the same.
- ***Edit:*** Look at the draft together. Have the tutee think about where improvements are necessary. The problem words, phrases or sentences can be marked with a coloured pen, pencil or highlighter. The most important area of need for improvement is where *meaning* is unclear. The second most important is to do with the organisation of ideas, or the *order* in which meanings are presented. Only then consider whether *spellings* are correct, and last of all whether *punctuation* is helpful and correct. The tutor can then make any additional suggestions about changes. Remember to use the dictionary, if in any doubt.
- ***Best Copy:*** It does not really matter who writes out the final best copy, because all the hard work is in the thinking before that stage. The tutor might do it, or the tutee, or both might do some, or someone else might word-process it from the edited and corrected draft. The best copy belongs to both tutor and tutee—both could sign it as authors.
- ***Evaluate:*** Perhaps later, the tutee and tutor inspect and evaluate their 'best copy'. 'Best copies' can be exchanged with other pairs for evaluation. Try to give more positive comments than critical comments. This should help the tutee think about how to improve next time.

MATHEMATICS: MAKE IT REAL AND SUMMARIZE

Question, make it real, check, summarise and generalise in mathematics.

Research Findings

The research evidence suggests that tutoring can be particularly effective in mathematics (*e.g.* Cohen, Kulik and Kulik, 1982). Britz (1989) reviewed studies of tutoring in mathematics published from 1980-89. Findings indicated the effectiveness of peer tutoring in promoting significant gains in mathematics performance for both the tutor and the tutee, including with low achievers, mildly handicapped or socially disadvantaged children. Heller and Fantuzzo (1993) have demonstrated the effectiveness of combining peer tutoring with parent tutoring in mathematics with 10-11 year-old students.

Tutoring in mathematics should not be just supervised mechanical drill. Tutors must not just do the problem for the tutee, or give them the answer. It is important that the tutee has time to talk and feels able to disclose their misunderstandings.

Mathematics is much more than just arithmetic. Its scope is so wide that some tutoring projects have used mathematical games (or other structured materials) to support the tutoring (*e.g.* Topping and Bamford, 1998*a*, 1998*b*). Designing a single tutoring procedure that could apply to all kinds of mathematics and requires no special materials is difficult. However, this has recently been done, based on principles of instructional design and the study of one-to-one interactions between professional teachers and students in mathematics. The resulting method is known as Duolog math (Topping, 2000*a*), on which the advice given here is based.

Practical Applications

- ***Listen:*** Give your tutee time to struggle to explain what their difficulty is. Do not just jump in to fix what you assume their difficulty is.
- ***Read:*** Your tutee might be having trouble reading a word problem. If so, read it for them and check their understanding.
- ***Question:*** Ask helpful and intelligent questions which give clues, to stimulate and guide student thinking, and challenge their misconceptions. Examples: 'what kind of problem is this?; 'what are we trying to find out here?; 'can we state the problem in different words or a different way?'; 'what *important* information do we already have?; 'can we break the problem into parts or

steps?; 'how did you arrive at that?; 'does that make sense?; 'where was the last place you knew you were right?; 'where do you think you might have gone wrong?; 'what kind of mistake do you think you might have made?' Do not say 'that's wrong!'— ask another question to give a clue. Ask 'why?' Try to avoid: Closed questions which require only a 'yes' or 'no' answer; questions which just rely on memory; questions which contain the answer; the question 'did you understand that?'. Try to avoid answering your own questions. Avoid indicating the 'difficulty' of any step.

- ***Pause for Think-aloud:*** Give your tutee some thinking time, before expecting an answer. Encourage them to tell you what they are thinking all the time. Then you will find out where and how they are going wrong. Remember tutors need time to think, also! If you are not sure, say so. You are not supposed to know everything.

- ***Make it Real:*** Try to make the problem seem real and related to the life of your tutee. Ask the tutee to try to imagine what the problem would *look* like in real life. Encourage them to use fingers, counters, cubes, sticks or any other objects to show the reality of the problem. Or have them draw dots, a picture, a list, table, diagram, graph or map. Useful charts include a number line, a multiplication matrix and a place-value chart. With your tutee's permission, mark their written working out with lines, arrows, colours or numbering to help them. Have the tutee think of what they have learned before or problems they have solved before, relevant to the current problem. Work through a similar but similar problem. How can this kind of problem be related to people, places, events and experiences in the home/community life of the tutee? Or those of someone they know or have seen on television? Make up a similar problem using the student's own name. Try to use everyday language.

- ***Check:*** Check that your tutee eventually gets the right answer. But remember there is probably more than one 'right' *way* to solve the problem. *Only if all else fails* show your tutee how you would do it (while *you* think aloud).

- ***Praise and Encourage:*** Give your tutee praise and encouragement very often, even for a very small success with a single step in solving a problem. Keep their confidence high.

- ***Summarize and Generalize:*** Have your tutee summarize the key strategies and steps in solving the problem. Point out any errors or gaps, then summarize the key strategies yourself. Talk about how these might be applied to another similar problem (generalized).

Recruit and Match Partners

Recruit and match learning partners with care.

Research Findings

The effects of different ways of recruiting tutors have not been systematically studied. In the United States of America, it is quite usual for tutors who are themselves students to receive course credit or payment for tutoring. In Europe, this is not at all usual, and there is much more emphasis on voluntary tutoring. Voluntary tutors might be assumed to be better motivated. But will their motivation last? This connects with the question of whether tutoring is seen as a substitute for professional teaching, or as a valuable, different and complementary experience in its own right.

The difference in ability between the tutor and the tutee is another issue. Some research suggests that tutoring by those who are very able in the subject is more beneficial to the tutee. However, tutoring at a level so far beneath their own might quickly become boring for the tutors, who are unlikely to obtain any stimulation or other intrinsic benefits. Tutoring in pairs with a much smaller difference in ability is likely to be much more challenging and engaging for the tutors. In this situation, the tutees might not gain so much, but the tutors are likely to gain in addition. In recent years there has been increased interest in the benefits of tutoring for the tutors. Also, near-ability tutors can be more credible models for tutees—they have themselves recently struggled and succeeded, showing that success is possible with effort (Cohen, Kulik and Kulik, 1982; Sharpley and Sharpley, 1981; Topping and Ehly, 1998).

The research suggests that age difference is much less important that ability difference, although the two might happen to go together. Research on gender differences has not yielded consistent findings, although there is some evidence that males benefit more than females from tutoring in some contexts, especially when serving as tutors to male tutees (Topping, 2000*b*). Of course, in some countries the idea of younger students tutoring older students, of females tutoring males (for example), might not be culturally acceptable.

Practical Applications

- ***Voluntary or Rewarded Tutors?*** Decide early on whether tutors will be rewarded or not, as it will effect recruitment—for good and/or bad.
- ***Parental Agreement:*** Consider whether parental agreement needs to be given, before tutoring commences.
- ***State Clear Goals:*** Tutor and tutee should agree on what they are trying to achieve. Do not be too ambitious.
- ***Say When You Do Not Know:*** Nobody knows everything. Tutors (and organisers of tutoring) should always say when they are unsure. Teaching something that is wrong harms both tutor and tutee.
- ***Decide Ability Differential:*** Are tutors and tutees to be quite close in ability in the subject of tutoring, or far apart? What are the advantages and disadvantages of each?
- ***Consider Personalities:*** Also think of possible personality and relationship clashes when matching pairs. For example, do not match a very quite and timid

tutee with a very dominant and strict tutor. Existing 'friends' might work well together—or they might chatter about anything but work. Do not necessarily accept tutee preference for a tutor.

- *Fixed or Reciprocal Roles:* Even in a pair of very different ability, sometimes it is effective for the tutee to try to teach the tutor something. This is a good way of checking if the tutee really understands it.
- *Schedule Contact Time:* How often will the pair meet each week? Where? How long will each session be? Over how many weeks? Both tutor and tutee must be clear about their time commitment.
- *Handling Absence:* Consider how to deal with the absence of tutor or tutee. You might wish to name a 'stand-by' tutor as back-up.

PROVIDE TRAINING AND MATERIALS

Specify tutoring method, provide training and access to materials.

Research Findings

Reviews of research on tutoring consistently find that more structured methods in which tutors receive training tend to yield better outcomes (Cohen, Kulik and Kulik, 1982; Sharpley and Sharpley, 1981; Topping and Ehly, 1998).

A clear procedure for tutoring needs to be specified. This can be generic (to be applied to any materials of the pair's choice). Or it might be based on, and structured by, some special materials the pair are given. If the method is to be applied to a wide range of materials, it is important to specify even more exactly what the tutor is to do (Topping, 2000*b*). For a first attempt, use of a 'packaged' method that has already been proved effective is recommended.

Even if tutoring is not based on given structured materials, pairs will still need access to some materials from which to choose (*e.g.* a collection of reading books). In developing countries, access to materials can be a big problem in some places.

Practical Applications

- *Specify Tutoring Method:* Be very clear about what good tutoring would look like. Perhaps use a 'packaged' technique? Consider general or specific tutoring skills, or some of both? Structured by specific materials, or not?
- *Training:* Train tutors and tutees together if possible. Tell them what to do. Then demonstrate what they have to do. Then give them a written and/or graphic reminder of what they have to do (to keep). Then have them immediately practice the tutoring method. Materials will be needed for practice. Observe and check whether they are doing it well. Give extra praise and coaching as needed.
- *Train in General Tutoring Skills:* For example, how to establish a comfortable relationship; how to present tasks; how to give clear explanations; how to ask questions; how to demonstrate skills; how to prompt or lead tutees into imitating skills; how to check on performance; how to give feedback and praise; how to identify consistent patterns of error; how to keep progress records.
- *Train in Specific Tutoring Skills:* As specifically relevant to your tutoring method and/or materials.
- *Contracting:* You might wish to have tutors and tutees sign some form of contract. This sets out the details of their agreement to work together.
- *Access to Materials:* These might be special materials that are specific to a tutoring programme. Or they might be regular classroom materials. Or materials publicly available (e.g. from a public library or downloaded from the Internet). If tutoring is based on 'homework' set by a teacher, the school is likely to provide the materials. Sometimes the materials are specially made. They can be produced by pairs themselves, or by volunteers or administrative staff under guidance. Pairs need to be able to obtain new materials before every tutoring session. Access must be frequent, quick and easy. Does that pair know what difficulty level to choose? What sequence to follow? How do they know?

MONITOR AND GIVE FEEDBACK

Monitor, give feedback and intervene to maximize effectiveness.

Research Findings

Reviews of research on tutoring consistently report effectiveness (Cohen, Kulik and Kulik, 1982; Sharpley and Sharpley, 1981; Topping and Ehly, 1998). However, even in the published literature (with its bias towards positive and statistically significant findings), a minority of tutoring projects do not show effectiveness. Tutoring can indeed be very effective, but that does not mean it is automatically effective everywhere.

To maximize effectiveness, start by using a structured method that has been reported as effective in the research literature. Be very careful and thorough in planning the tutoring, training the tutors and tutees, and providing appropriate materials. Then (equally importantly) monitor the implementation of the tutoring and give feedback and intervene where needed (Topping, 2000*b*).

Practical Applications

- ***Goals of Monitoring:*** Seek to: detect and solve any problems before they become large; find opportunities to give plentiful praise and show enthusiasm to keep motivation high; ensure the tutoring technique does not show signs of 'drift'; check that pairs are maintaining positive social relationships; be sure that materials used are from an appropriate sequence/level of difficulty; and generally review the complexity and richness of the learning taking place.
- ***Self-help Guide:*** Make a simple self-help guide of common problems in tutoring, with suggestions about how these might be solved. You will keep adding to this. With 'packaged' techniques, clues about likely problems will be found in the literature.
- ***Self-referral:*** Let tutors and tutees know it is usual for many pairs to encounter some temporary difficulty, so this is not the fault of either helper or helped. They

should know who to ask if one or both have any difficulty (with a particular problem, the tutoring technique or each other). They could seek help from other pairs before approaching a teacher.

- ***Self-recording:*** The pair should record their progress, and a monitoring teacher or tutoring organiser can then check these records or diaries from time to time.
- ***Discussion:*** Talk with the tutors and tutees about how things are going, perhaps at 'planning' or 'de-briefing' meetings. You might do this individually or in groups, with tutors and tutees together or separate.
- ***Direct Observation:*** Carefully observe tutoring as it happens. (Do not assume that even the most intelligent tutor will be aware if they are going wrong.) A checklist of the elements of the tutoring technique will be helpful to structure these observations consistently. You could also ask 'spare' tutors to monitor sometimes, using this checklist. It is possible to use video or audio recording for monitoring, and this can be useful for feedback to individual pairs or the group as a whole, as well as being valuable as a training aid for subsequent projects.
- ***Further Training:*** If several pairs are having problems, it is probably worth holding another 'refresher' training session.

Conclusion

Tutoring can be very effective. But it is not automatically effective. Parents who try to tutor their own child at home sometimes become frustrated and bad-tempered. Parents might also tutor the way they were taught at school, which might be quite different to the way the subject is taught in school today. So there are especial dangers when parents try to 'help' children with homework, especially when the children are older and their schoolwork is more advanced. Take care, and discuss exactly how you can help with your child's school teachers.

You might feel that all the advice given in this booklet makes tutoring seem very complicated. Be reassured—it is not so difficult, really. Make a start and learn for yourself as you go along. Many of the potential problems will never happen. But at least now you are prepared for anything. Well, almost anything.

This booklet is only a starting place. References and suggestions for further reading are found in the following section.

After you have read this booklet, try hard to find an opportunity to observe tutoring in action. Think about the good and bad points of what you saw. How many of the 'Principles' in this booklet were being followed? How many were being broken?

Discuss the ideas in the booklet with your friends and colleagues. Try out a tutoring programme. Discuss what happens with your partners, colleagues and friends. Then teach someone else some of what you have learned. Then you will *really* have learned it.

REFERENCES

Bloom, B.S. 1984. The Search for Methods of Group Instruction as Effective as One-to-One Tutoring. *Educational Leadership* (Alexandria, VA), Vol. 41, No. 8, p. 4-17.

Britz, M.W. 1989. The effects of peer tutoring on mathematics performance: A recent review. *British Journal of Special Education* (Oxford, UK), Vol. 13, No. 1, p. 17-33.

Brooks, G., et al. 1998. *What Works for Slow Readers? The Effectiveness of Early Intervention Schemes*. Slough, UK, National Foundation for Educational Research.

Brophy, J.E. 1981. Teacher Praise: A Functional Analysis, *Review of Educational Research* (Washington, DC), Vol. 51, p. 5-32.

Cohen, P.A.; Kulik, J.A.; Kulik, C-L.C. 1982. Educational Outcomes of Tutoring: A Meta-Analysis of Findings. *American Educational Research Journal* (Washington, DC), Vol. 19, No. 2, p. 237-48.

Daiute, C. 1989. Play As Thought: Thinking Strategies of Young Writers. *Harvard Educational Review* (Cambridge, MA), Vol. 59, No. 1, p. 1-23.

—, 1990. The Role of Play in Writing Development. *Research in the Teaching of English* (Urbana, IL), Vol. 24, No. 1, p. 4-47.

Daiute, C.; Dalton, B. 1993. Collaboration Between Children Learning to Write: Can Novices be Masters? *Cognition and Instruction* (Hillsdale NJ), Vol. 10, No. 4, p. 281-333.

Devin-Sheehan, L.; Feldman, R.S.; Allen, V.L. 1976. Research on Children Tutoring Children: A Critical Review. *Review of Educational Research* (Washington, DC), Vol. 46, No. 4, p. 355-85.

Fuchs, D.; Fuchs, L.S. 1998. Researchers and Teachers Working Closely Together to Adapt Instruction for Diverse Learners. *Learning Disability Research and Practice* (Mahwah, NJ), Vol, 13, p. 126-137.

Gage, N.L.; Berliner, D. 1998. *Educational Psychology*, 6th Edition, Boston, Houghton and Mifflin.

Good, T.L.; Brophy, J.E. 1995. *Contemporary Educational Psychology*, 5th Edition. New York, Longman.

Heller, L.R.; Fantuzzo, J.W. 1993. Reciprocal Peer Tutoring and Parent Partnership: Does Parent Involvement Make a Difference? *School Psychology Review* (Silver Spring, MD), Vol. 22, No. 3, p. 517-34.

Levine, H.M.; Glass, G.V.; Meister, G.R. 1987. A Cost-Effectiveness Analysis of Computer-Assisted Instruction. *Evaluation Review* (Thousand Okas, CA), Vol. 11. No. 1, p. 50-72.

Nixon, J.; Topping, K.J. In Press. Emergent Writing: The Impact of Structure Peer Interaction. *Educational Psychology* (Abingdon, UK), Vol. 21, no. 1.

O' Donnell, A.M; Topping, K.J. 1998. Peers Assessing Peers: Possibilities and Problems. *In:* Topping, K.J.; Ehly, S., eds. *Peer-Assisted Learning*. Marwah, NJ; London, Lawrence Erlbaum Associates.

Rohrbeck, C., et. al. 1999. *Peer-Assisted Learning Interventions: A Meta-Analysis*. Paper Presented At the Annual Conference of the American Psychological Association. Washington, DC, 22 August 1999.

Sharpley, A.M.; Sharpley, C.F. 1981. Peer Tutoring: A Review of the Literature. *Collected Original Resources in Education (CORE)* (Abingdon, UK), Vol. 5, No. 3, 7-C11 (Fiches 7 and 8).

Sutherland, J.A.; Topping, K.J. 1999. Collaborative Creative Writing in Eight-Year-Olds: Comparing Cross-Ability Fixed Role and Same-Ability Reciprocal Role Pairing. *Journal of Research in Reading* (Oxford, UK), Vol. 22, No. 2, p. 154-179.

Topping, K.J. 1992. Short-and long-term follow-up of Parental Involvement in Reading Projects. *British Educational Research Journal* (Oxford, UK), Vol. 18, No. 4, p. 369-79.

— 1995. *Paired Reading, Spelling and Writing. The Handbook for Teachers and Parents*. London; New York, Cassell.

—, 2000*a*. *Duolog Math: Design of a Generic Tutoring Procedure in Mathematics*. Dundee, Centre for Paired Learning, University of Dundee.

—. 2000*b*. *Peer Assisted Learning: A Practical Guide for Teachers*. Cambridge, MA, Brookline Books.

—. 2001. *Thinking, Reading, Writing: A Practical Guide to Paired Learning With Peers, Parents and Volunteers*. New York; London, Continuum International.

Topping, K.J.; Bamford, J. 1998*a*. *The Paired Maths Handbook: Parental Involvement and Peer Tutoring in Mathematics*. London, Fulton; Bristol, PA, Taylor and Francis.

—, —, 1998*b*. *Parental Involvement and Peer Tutoring in Mathematics and Science*. Developing Paired Maths into Paired Science. London, Fulton; Bristol, PA, Taylor and Francis.

Topping, K.J.; Ehly, S., eds. 1998. *Peer-Assisted Learning*. Mahwah, NJ; London, Lawrence Erlbaum Associates.

Topping, K.J.; Lindsay, G.A. 1992. Paired Reading: A Review of the Literature. *Research Papers in Education* (London), Vol. 7, No. 3, p. 199-246.

Topping, K.J; Whiteley, M. 1990. Participant Evaluation of Parent-tutored and Peer-Tutored Projects in Reading. *Educational Research* (London), Vol. 32, No. 1, p. 14-32.

Walberg, H.J.; Haertel, G.D., eds. 1997. *Psychology and Educational Practice*. Berkeley, CA, McCutchan Publishing.

Wasik, B.A.; Slavin, R.E. 1993. Preventing Early Reading Failure With One-to-One Tutoring: A Review of Five Programs. *Reading Research Quarterly* (Newark, DE), Vol. 28, No. 2, p. 178-200.

Yarrow, F.; Topping, K.J. In Press. Collaborative Writing: The Effects of Metacognitive Promoting and Structured Peer Interaction. *British Journal of Educational Psychology* (Letchworth, UK).

Further Reading

(N.B. Advice Given by Other Authors Might not be Evidence-Based)

Aldrich, S.; Wright, J. Undated. *Peer Tutoring: A Multimedia Manual*. Syracuse, NY, Syracuse City School District. Available From: www.scsd.k12.ny.us/sbit/dirhtml/libfile/libdocs/software/peertut.pdf [1 August 2000]. (Acrobat Reader Required.)

Capossela, T. 1998. *The Harcourt Brace Guide to Peer Tutoring*. Foth Worth, TX, Harcourt Brace College Publishers.

Ender, S.C.; Newton, F.B. 2000. *Students Helping Students: A Guide for Peer Educators on College Campuses*. San Francisco, CA, Jossey-Bass.

Gillespie, P.; Lerner, N. 1999. *The Allyn and Bacon Guide to Peer Tutoring*. Boston, MA, Allyn and Bacon.

Johnston, F.R.; Invernizzi, M.; Juel, C. 1998. *Book Buddies: Guidelines for Volunteer Tutors of Emergent and Early Readers*. New York, Guilford Press.

Morris, D. 1999. *The Howard Street Tutoring Manual: Teaching at-Risk Readers in the Primary Grades*. New York, Guilford Press.

Topping, K.J. 1995. *Paired Reading, Spelling and Writing: The Handbook for Teachers and Parents*. London; New York, Cassell.

——, 2000. *Peer Assisted Learning: A Practical Guide for Teachers* Cambridge, MA, Brookline Books.

——, 2001. *Thinking, Reading, Writing: A Practical Guide to Paired Learning with Peers, Parents and Volunteers*. New York; London, Continuum International.

Topping, K.J.; Ehly, S., eds. 1998. *Peer-Assisted Learning*. Mahwah, NJ; London, Lawrence Erlbaum Associates.

In Languages Other Than English

Cupolillo, M., et al. 1998. Lectura Conjunta: Proyecto Realizado Con Alumnos Que Repetian Primer Grado En La Escuela Publica Brasilena. *Lectura Y Vida* (Buenos Aires), Vol. 19, No. 4, p. 21-29.

Topping, K.J. 1989. Lactura Conjunta: Una Poderosa Técnica Al Servicio De Los Padres. *Communicación, Lenguaje Y Educación* (Madrid), No. 3-4, p. 143-151.

——, 1997. *Tutoring: Insegnamento Reciproco Tra Compagni*. Trento, Erickson.

Courtesy: UNESCO's International Bureau of Education and International Academy of Education.

5

Teaching Additional Languages

*Elliot L. Judd**
*Lihua Tan***
*Herbert J, Walberg****

Introduction

For several reasons, we have chosen the last two words in this chapter's title. 'Teaching additional languages' rather than commonly used terms 'second languages' or 'foreign languages'. Students may actually be learning not a second but a third or fourth language. 'Additional' applies to all, except, of course, the first language learned. An additional language, moreover, may not be foreign since many people in their country may ordinarily speak it. The term 'foreign' can, moreover, suggest strange, exotic or, perhaps, alien—all undesirable connotations. Our choice of the term 'additional' underscores our belief that additional languages are not necessarily inferior nor superior nor a replacement for a student's first language.

Our view is that students should be taught how to use an additional language clearly, accurately and effectively for *genuine* communication. They should read and listen to live language;

---

* University of Illinois of Chicago, United States of America.
** Guizhou University of Technology, People's Republic of China.
*** University of Illinois at Chicago, United States of America.

they should speak and write it in ways that can be understood by native and non-native speakers. Learners, moreover, should eventually to be able to produce and comprehend additional languages independently without the aid of a teacher.

We begin by presenting some key general principles of such 'communicative language' teaching and follow with principles about particular kinds of teaching. In each case, we briefly summarize the research, and then discuss classroom practices that follow from it. At the end of each section is a list of suggested readings that expand on what has been presented, and provide additional principles, research and classroom activities.

Comprehensible Input

Learners need exposure to lots of meaningful and understandable language.

Research Findings

Comprehensible input refers to meaningful oral and written language somewhat above the learners' current level of mastery. Such input allows for the acquisition of grammar and vocabulary, which, in turn, makes exposure to additional input more comprehensible. Mere exposure to language is insufficient. Learners must take notice of key features in order for comprehensible input to be beneficial. Although such input is necessary, it is insufficient, as discussed in the next section on opportunities for interaction.

In the Classroom

Several classroom-teaching strategies derive from the idea of comprehensible input:

- Teachers should expose their students to listening and reading materials that are somewhat above their current language proficiency levels;
- Students should be asked to understand the material, not merely to reproduce it;
- Teachers should focus the students' attention on key grammar and vocabulary items;

- Students should be asked to guess the meaning of the input based on their prior knowledge of the topic, and on other known words and concepts within the next;
- Teachers should try to create situations within and outside the classroom that expose students to sources of comprehensible input.

LANGUAGE OPPORTUNITIES

Classroom activities should allow students to use natural and meaningful language with their classmates.

Research Findings

Learners need opportunities to practice language with one another. Conversations are important since they require attentiveness and involvement on the part of learners. By conversing, they can practise adapting vocabulary and grammar to a particular situation and making their own contributions to the conversation comprehensible.

The best conversations for such learning exchange real information, ideas and feelings among the participants. By engaging in such activities, learners have opportunities to try to make themselves understood. They receive immediate feedback as to whether they were successful and where alternative language is needed. As they engage in such exchanges, learners also receive additional comprehensible input, which further aids language acquisition.

In the Classroom

Several classroom-teaching strategies derive from these research findings:

- Teachers should go beyond simple language drills to create opportunities for meaningful interaction in the classroom by using activities in which students employ natural language examples in real language situations;
- Students should be encouraged to work in pairs or small groups, with the teacher serving as an occasionally helpful observer rather than a controlling force.

- Teachers should employ activities in which students have to solve problems in which each party must contribute information that others do not possess and which challenge students' minds;
- When feasible, the tasks should relate to students' needs and interests so as to motivate them;
- Teachers should usually avoid intervening in these activities while they are occurring, but should provide feedback after they conclude.

LANGUAGE PRACTICE

Classroom activities should encourage students to use the additional language for genuine communication.

Research Findings

Communicative-language teaching employs activities that prepare students for natural, appropriate additional-language use outside the classroom. Language is viewed as more than grammar drills are word memorization. The goal is to train students in language skills that enable them to function easily by themselves without their teachers. Students need to learn what language is effective and culturally appropriate in natural discourse. Errors in additional-language learning are a natural part of learning, but they should be detected and corrected early. Supervised by their teachers, students can practice with one another and detect and correct each other's errors.

The teacher's role is not to control and dominate the classroom. Instead, the teacher can present real-language models to the students (comprehensible input), provide information and focus to the language forms being studied, use a limited amount of controlled exercises so that students gain confidence, and then allow students in interact with each other by using language for natural communicative functions. Thus, the classroom should be neither completely learner-centred nor completely teacher-controlled; rather both contribute to learning. In addition to the general classroom implications below, we have included more specific teaching strategies in the section that follow.

In the Classroom

Teachers should not only use traditional language drills in the classroom; they should also:

- Employ freer, open-ended activities (with more than one possible solution) that allow students to experiment with language to develop oral and written fluency.
- Use materials that represent real, natural language, not artificially constructed textbook language that presents patterns that no speaker would ever use in natural situations. The learning tasks presented by the instructor should mirror real-life language use.
- Provide meaningful feedback to students on how they performed the communicative activities and provide suggestions for improvement. Feedback should first focus on how well the students did on the communicative aspects of the task and then on the forms used by the student.

Learning Strategies

Students should be taught strategies that enable them to increasingly learn language on their own and from their classmates and others without their teacher's help.

Research Findings

Classes cannot allow enough time to teach everything about additional languages. If students are taught how to learn on their own, they can acquire vocabulary and language skills by themselves without their teachers. Successful strategies include taking a slow breath to reduce anxiety, raising pertinent questions about difficult points, and being sensitive to the difficulties of others. Other strategies are tricks to memorize words, guessing and then checking meanings, and maximizing opportunities for language practice.

In the Classroom

Teachers can employ several techniques for encouraging language-learning strategies:

- Observe students to see which learning strategies lead to better learning.
- Instruct students in strategies that can help them successfully learn and which allow them to become independent.
- Be aware of learners' emotions and use techniques to reduce their anxiety.
- Encourage students to share successful strategies with each other.
- Teach students strategies that can help them compensate when they do not understand or cannot think of a word or phrase.

LISTENING

Students should be given practice in understanding naturally spoken additional languages.

Research Findings

Students need to comprehend natural spoken language—in lectures, the media (radio, cinema and television), and in face-to-face conversations. Many students have a greater need to understand than to speak an additional language. Listening is crucial for language acquisition because it provides 'comprehensible input' (previously discussed).

How do we comprehend spoken language? One model is called 'bloom-up' processing. According to this view, we piece together a message by first understanding the smallest units of language—sounds. Then, we connect the sounds together to form words. Our knowledge of words enables us to understand phrases, then sentences, and finally entire passages. An alternative view is known as a 'top-down' approach. In this model, based on our knowledge of the topic and situation, we can figure out the specific meaning of a passage; and the sentences, phrases and words that form the message.

Current theory suggests an 'interactive' model, in which listeners simultaneously use both top-down and bottom-up strategies. One strategy compensates for gaps in the other, until the entire message is understood.

There are many types of listening. Sometimes we listen for the general meaning of a message, sometimes for specific information. At times listening is a one-way process (e.g. a lecture or a movie, and at other times it is two-way and involves both listening and speaking as in a conversation. Some listening entails mainly information exchange; other listening may be more social and emotional in which feelings are more prominent.

In the Classroom

For listening comprehension, the following teaching strategies can be recommended:

- Before listening to a passage, ask students what they know about the topic in order to remind them of their prior knowledge. A teacher may also preview difficult vocabulary and ideas prior to listening;
- Following the listening, ask students about the general points of the passage;
- In details are to be recalled, allow students to take notes.
- Use natural language for listening passages. It is better to use short pieces or real language at the beginning levels than artificial teacher-made language;
- Use a variety of different listening activities such as one-way and two-way, and informational and emotional.

SPEAKING

Students should be given practice speaking in language comprehensible to others.

Research Finding

Additional language instruction formerly consisted of students' memorizing dialogues and practising grammar drills. Current research supports a model known as 'communicative competence'. Although students must learn the grammar and vocabulary, these alone do not lead to fluency. Since natural language is unpredictable and speakers arrive at meaning through active communication, students must be taught how to manage real conversation—how to start and end conversations, how to respond appropriately, and how to express their beliefs, opinions and feelings. Students need to learn what is culturally appropriate and how language varies depending on the situations; they may need to learn about people involved, their moods, and other social and cultural factors. A fluent speaker needs to know how to link utterances together to create clear and effective discourse.

Students must also learn how to manage conversations when there are communication breakdowns. These modern views caused changes in the teaching of speaking. Students should engage in 'unscripted' or spontaneous language since that is the nature of usual speaking practices. The teacher's role is to provide language patterns that are needed, guide students in how to form natural language, and then to create opportunities for practice. Teachers must provide judicious coaching and encouragement so that students will actively practice speaking.

In the Classroom

When teaching speaking, the following instructional strategies are recommended:

- Present to students the linguistic and vocabulary patterns and make sure they understand how they are formed, when they are used, and their cultural implications;
- Teach students speech acts (to agree/disagree, apologize, make excuses, etc.), forms to manage conversations (openings, interruptions, closing, etc.) and strategies for round-about speaking when they don't know a specific word;
- Provide controlled practice so students can feel comfortable with the patterns;
- Have students use the patterns in natural language situations that are relevant to their speaking needs.

Pretending they are asking for directions or requesting a hotel room are examples.

- Allow the students to make errors, but also provide feedback on what is successful and unsuccessful.

Reading

Students should be given practice in comprehending natural texts.

Research Findings

The ability to read ordinary texts in an additional language is a crucial skill that students should master. Reading, like listening, is an interactive process. Students need to master bottom-up skills: recognizing letters, understanding words and phrases, and comprehending sentences (see Principle 5). At the same time, top-down knowledge is important in reading comprehension. Background knowledge enables readers to understand a passage, and to make a sensible guess when a word or phrase is not understood. Efficient readers make use of both top-down and bottom-up strategies; they use one to compensate for lack of knowledge of the other. Therefore, teachers need to provide instruction in both types of strategies in a comprehensive reading programme.

Skilled readers can also adapt their speed to their purpose and the text. Sometimes they read an entire passage carefully and slowly seeking the main ideas, detailed information, and inferences and implications. Sometimes they quickly scan a text to find out the major points or to answer a single question. Such tasks need to be taught. To acquire them, students need to read a wide variety of naturally occurring texts: both literary and non-literary, academic and non-academic, formal and informal. Thus, a reading programme should not only use traditional reading passages, but also contain such things as maps, schedules, menus and signs. Finally, a course in reading should include both intensive reading, which is done in classroom situations and emphasizes specific reading skills, and more extensive reading done by students outside of class, which provides additional reading opportunities.

In the Classroom

Following from these research findings are several general teaching strategies:

- Teach bottom-up reading skills, such as rapidly processing common words and phrases, and call attention to rhetorical markers such as 'however' and 'therefore';
- Refresh background knowledge before reading a passage;
- Use natural language texts and select material that corresponds to the various types of readings that students will encounter;
- Teach appropriate reading strategies that correspond to the texts and real-life tasks: reading for general meaning, recalling specific information, understanding inferences and implications, skimming, scanning, etc.;
- Provide numerous opportunities for reading, both inside and outside of classes.

WRITING

Students should be given practice in creating effective, natural language that communicates their intended message.

Research Findings

Two major approaches to the teaching of writing have been under discussion for some time. The first, known as the 'product approach', fucuses on the final outcome of writing, which is a logical, error-free essay. Students are given a model text, which they study, analyse and then reproduce. Different models are presented for different types of writing.

In contrast is the 'process approach' to writing, which emphasizes the steps a writer goes through when creating a well-written text. Among the stages taught are: *brainstorming* or writing down may ideas that may come to an individual's mind; *outlining*, which organises the ideas into a logical sequence; *drafting*, in which the writer concentrates on the content of the message rather than the form; *revisions* in response to the writer's second thoughts or feedback provided by peers or teachers; *proof-reading* with an emphasis on form; and the *final draft*. All of the processes should be explained, taught and practised by the students.

Some recent research suggests the value of focusing on various writing 'genres' in an effort to identify, compare and contrast writings in different fields, such as science and literature. Rather than three incompatible approaches, a writing programme should integrate product, process and genre writing into a coherent whole. In addition, many students may need special practice in non-academic materials—letters, forms, resumés, lists, etc. These, too, might be appropriately included in writing classes.

In the Classroom

The following are some suggestions for teaching writing:

- Teach students the stages to writing: brainstorming, writing a first draft, revising, editing, etc.
- Provide models of successful writing samples and discuss the features that make them effective;
- Discuss audience expectations of acceptable writing and how different genres use different writing styles;
- Select writing topics that are of interest to the students and represent tasks that students will need to master in future writing;
- Teach students real-life writing tasks like filling out forms, letters, charts, etc.

Grammar

Formal grammar instruction may have some benefits in certain situations, but may be of limited benefit in others.

Research Findings

In traditional additional language courses, teachers spent much time concentrating on formal grammar. Yet, mere presentation of grammatical forms in isolation, followed by drills may not lead to correct use and students may continue making grammatical errors when trying to communicate. Current research suggests that language teaching needs to be more than grammar instruction. Learners need to understand the meaning of the form, as well as the discourse in which the form appears. Students, moreover, may need to practise and master some vocabulary before they can appreciate and benefit from explicit instruction in grammar. It is then, after an error occurs, that the teacher's corrective feedback may be most beneficial.

In the Classroom

The following are basic procedures for teaching a grammatical pattern:

- Present the grammar form in natural discourse, explaining how the form is made, any irregular forms, and any spelling or pronunciation issues;
- Provide numerous examples of natural language in which the form can be studied and provide any contextual information on how to use the form appropriately;
- Make sure the students can recognize the form and its functions, before asking the students to produce the form;
- Provide activities that allow students to use the form in natural communicative ways, not just in simple drills;
- If errors occur, provide meaningful feedback on what forms should be used and why, but remember it often takes time for students to master a form completely.

Comprehensible Pronunciation

Pronunciation instruction should make students understandable to other users of an additional language.

Research Findings

Researchers have debated whether it is possible for older additional-language learners to obtain a native-like accent. Most agree that few such students can achieve a native-like accent.

For most communication purposes, it is generally unimportant to do so. Students need to develop the ability to be understood by other speakers, not to sound like a native. Pronunciation must be comprehensible and not detect from the understanding of a message. Thus, teachers must work on the pronunciation of individual sounds, both vowels and consonants and on the various sound combinations.

Of equal importance is teaching the intonation, stress and rhythm patterns of the additional language, which often block effective communication. Inability in these areas causes more communication problems than the inaccurate pronunciation of individual sounds.

In teaching pronunciation, students need practice in natural contexts. Feedback is an essential part of pronunciation instruction, since students may not be able to evaluate how successful they are in creating the pattern. When selecting a pronunciation feature, the instructor should illustrate how native language patterns may facilitate or hinder communication in the additional language.

In the Classroom

Several teaching strategies should be helpful in teaching pronunciation:

- Teach students to listen carefully to pronunciation. Often contrasting it with another pattern will enable them to recognize the important differences;
- Encourage students to use the pattern in isolation and then in natural sentence contexts;
- Students should also use the pattern in sentences of their own making;
- Teach students to produce correct intonation, stress and rhythm;
- Learning pronunciation is difficult and takes time. Difficult pattern may need re-teaching.

Conclusion

In closing this brief account of effective additional language teaching, three points deserve emphasis:

- The various language skills discussed above should be integrated in realistic language situations. In preparing a report, for example, students may need to read and write. They may also need to discuss their ideas with their peers, which entails listening and speaking. Imagining particular language situations may make it clear how to integrate the various language skills;
- Since useful language facility requires comprehension and fluency in ordinary, non-academic settings, paper-and-and-pencil tests will ordinarily be insufficient by themselves. A broader approach would include assessment of students' comprehension of a variety of naturally spoken language passages and ability to respond fluently in conversations;
- In designing and teaching courses for additional languages, educators should assess students' prior language abilities and cultural experience, their specific language needs, the situations in which they will use the additional language, and the proficiency level expected. From this assessment, they can select appropriate course material and activities that are authentic, motivating and challenging.

REFERENCES

Aebersold, J.; Field, M. 1997. *From Reader to Reading: Issues and Strategies in Second Language Classrooms*. Cambridge, United Kingdom, Cambridge University Press.

Anderson, N. 1999. *Secondary-Language Reading: Issues and Strategies*. Boston, MA, Heinle and Heinle.

Brown, G. 1992. *Listening to Spoken Language*. 2nd ed. London, Longman.

Brown, G.; Yule, G. 1983. *Teaching the Spoken Language*. Cambridge, United Kingdom, Cambridge University Press.

Brumfit, C. 1984. *Communicative Methodology in Language Teaching*. Cambridge, United Kingdom, Cambridge University Press.

Bygate, M. 1987. *Speaking*. Oxford, United Kingdom, Oxford University Press.

Campbell, C. 1999. *Teaching Second-Language Writing: Interacting with Text*. Boston, MA, Heinle and Heinle.

Celce-Murcia, M. 1991. *Teaching English as A Second or Foreign Language*. 2nd ed. New York, Newbury House.

——, 1991. Grammar Pedagogy in Second-and Foreign-Language Teaching. *TESOL Quarterly* (Alexandria, VA), No. 25, p. 459-80.

Celce-Murica, M.; Brinton D.; Goodwin, J. 1996. *Teaching Pronunciation: A Reference for Teaching of English to Speakers of Other Languages*. Cambridge, United Kingdom, Cambridge University Press.

Celce-Murcia, M.; Larsen-Freeman, D. 1999. *The Grammar Book: An ESL/ EFL Teacher's Guide*. 2nd ed. Boston, MA, Heinle and Heinle.

Day, R.; Bamford J. 1998. *Extensive Reading in the Second-Language Classroom*. Cambridge, United Kingdom, Cambridge University Press.

Doughty, C.; Pica T. 1986. 'Information Gap' Tasks: Do They Facilitate Second-Language Acquisition? *TESOL Quarterly* (Alexandria, VA), No. 20, p. 305-25.

Ellis, R. 1988. *Classroom Second-Language Development*. London, Prentice Hall.

——, 1990. *Instructed Language Acquisition*. London, Blackwell.

Ferris, D.; Hedgcock, J. 1998. *Teaching ESL Composition: Purpose, Process and Practice*. Hillsdale, NJ, Erlbaum.

Hadley, A. 1993. *Teaching Language in Context*. Boston, MA, Heinle and Heinle.

Kenworthy, J. 1987. *Teaching English Pronunciation*. London, Longman.

Krashen, S. 1982. *Principles and Practices in Second-Language Acquisition*. Oxford, Pergamon.

Lightbown, P.; Spada, N. 1993. *How Language are Learned*. Oxford, United Kingdom, Oxford University Press.

Long, M.; Porter, P. 1985. Group Work, Interlanguage Tasks and Second-Language Acquisition. *TESOL Quarterly* (Alexandria, VA), No,. 19, p. 207-27.

McCarthy, M.; Carter, R. 1994. *Language as Discourse: Perspective for Language Teachers*. London, Longman.

Mendelsohn, D. 1994. *Learning to Listen*. San Diego, CA, Domine Press.

Morley, J. 1994. *Pronunciation Pedagogy and Theory: New Views, New Dimensions*. Alexandria, VA. TESOL.

Nunan, D. 1991. *Language Teaching Methodology*. London, Prentice-Hall.

——, 1999. *Second Language Teaching and Learning*. Boston, MA, Heinle and Heinle.

O'Malley, J.; Chamot, A. 1990. *Learning Strategies in Second-Language Acquisition*. Cambridge, United Kingdom, Cambridge University Press.

Oxford, R. 1990. *Language Learning Strategies: What Every Teacher Should know*. New York, Newbury House/Harper and Row.

Reid, J. 1993. *Teaching ESL Writing*. Englewood Cliffs, NJ, Prentice-Hall/ Regents.

Rust, M. 1990. *Listening in Language Learning*. London. Longman.

Savignon, S. 1991. Communicative Language Teaching: State of the Art. *TESOL quarterly* (Alexandria, VA), No. 25, p. 261-77.

Wendon, A. 1991. *Learner Strategies for Learner Autonomy*. Englewood Cliffs, NJ, Prentice-Hall.

Williams, J. 1995. Focus on Form in Communicative Language Teaching: Research Findings and the Classroom Teacher. *TESOL JOURNAL* (Alexandria, VA), Vol. 4, No. 4, p. 12-16.

Courtesy: UNESCO's International Bureau of Education and International Academy of Education.

6

Motivation To Learn

*Prof. Monique Boekaerts**

Introduction

In the last forty years, researchers have studied student motivation and have learned a great deal about:

- What moves students to learn and the quantity and quality of the effort they invest;
- What choices students make;
- What makes them persist in the face of hardship;
- How student motivation is affected by teacher practices and peer behaviour;
- How motivation develops;
- How the school environment affects it.

Most of the motivation research focused on well-adjusted students who are successful in school. However, successful students differ from their less-successful peers in many ways. For example, they often have clear ideas of what they want and do not want to achieve in life. Moreover, they perceive many learning settings as supportive of their own wishes, goals and needs, and react positively to the teacher's motivational practices.

* Leiden University, Netherlands.

This booklet is a synthesis of principles of motivation that have emerged from research into the effect of motivational practices on school learning. It addresses more traditional aspects, such as achievement motivation, intrinsic motivation and goal orientation, as well as the effect of teacher practices that promote motivational beliefs, motivation strategies and willpower. It focuses on learning goals and the effect of motivation on the pursuit of these goals, whilst recognizing the need for teacher practices that target socio-emotional goals as well.

Much of the research supporting the principles specified in this booklet stems from studies that investigated the association between motivation (seen as a student characteristic) and learning outcomes. Other principles have their origins in the theory of self that children and adolescents themselves develop through the years. Still other principles are based on research that showed how the opportunities that teachers and schools provide for learning and personal development (instructional procedures, teacher behaviour and classroom climate) are congruent or in conflict with the students' needs and goals. Priority was given to those principles that teachers can apply in their classrooms. It is the aim of this short introduction to motivation to make teachers aware that youngsters' psychological needs change continuously. They change not just as a function of their developing knowledge and expertise in a particular subject-matter domain, but also in relation to their emerging theory of self in relation to that domain.

In this booklet, the reader will get to know two youngsters, namely Stefano and Sandra, who are both 11 years old and are attending school in different parts of the world. Stefano is the son of a car mechanic. He goes to school in a rural area in the south of Europe. Sandra is the daughter of a road worker. She attends school in a big city in South America. It is my intention to describe the thoughts, feelings and actions of these two children in order to provide and illustration of the various constructs described in the research sections. I hope that teachers will perceive these students' developing values, interests and goals as similar to what they actually observe in their own classrooms.

The eight principles addressed in this booklet are meant to be understood as pieces in a jug-saw puzzle that fit together to provide a coherent, comprehensive picture of how to provide a powerful environment for motivation strategies to develop. If you want to find out more about these eight principles, or about a specific principle, you can consult the literature on motivation. References are provided in relation to each principle.

Motivational Beliefs

Motivational beliefs act as favourable contexts for learning.

Research Findings

In the classroom the content covered and the social context vary continuously. Hence, children are frequently involved in unfamiliar learning situations. This may create ambiguity and uncertainty for some students and challenge for other students. Students try to make sense of novel learning situations by referring to their motivational beliefs. Motivational beliefs refer to the opinions, judgements and values that students hold about objects, events or subject-matter domains. Researchers have described the beliefs that students use to assign meaning to learning situations. A specific set of motivational beliefs pertains to the value students attach to a domain. For example, Stefano often says: 'I cannot see what I can possibly learn from reading poetry;' while Sandra states: 'Reading poems is the nicest activity we do at school.'

Motivational beliefs also refer to the student's opinion of the efficiency or effectiveness of learning and teaching methods (Stefano: 'Why do we always have to work in groups? I can learn better when I work alone'). Beliefs about internal control can be distinguished into self-efficacy beliefs and outcome expectations. Self-efficiency beliefs are opinions that students hold about their own ability in relation to a specific domain (Stefano: 'I believe that I am good at solving this type of mathematics problem;' Sandra: 'I am not a star in math, but I know how to analyze a reading text'). Outcome expectations are beliefs about the success or failure of specific actions (Stefano: 'I have been working at this grammar task for a long time and I still cannot get it right. I am certain I will not be able to come up with an acceptable solution').

Research has indicated that motivational beliefs result from direct learning experiences (*e.g.* Sandra: 'Most math problems are too difficult for me to get them right the first time. However, when somebody gives me a hint I can solve a lot of problems'), observation learning (*e.g.* Stefano: 'The math teacher gets annoyed when students do not offer help to each other'), verbal statements by teachers, parents or peers (*e.g.* Sandra: 'My father thinks it is nonsense to learn poetry in school; he says mathematics is far more important') and social comparisons (*e.g.* Stefano: 'Why do I always get scolded, while the teacher never says anything to other students?').

Motivational beliefs act as a frame of reference that guides students' thinking, feelings and actions in a subject area. For example, motivational beliefs about mathematics determine which strategies students think are appropriate to do specific tasks. It is noteworthy that a student's beliefs about a domain may be dominantly favourable (optimistic) or unfavourable (pessimistic), thus providing a positive or negative context for learning. Once formed, favourable and unfavourable motivational beliefs are very resistant to change.

Motivating Your Students

As teachers, you should have a good idea of the motivational beliefs that your students bring into the classroom. It is important that you are aware that your students may already have formed favourable or unfavourable beliefs about a topic before they come into class. Knowledge about your students' motivational beliefs will allow you to plan learning activities that make good use of their favourable motivational beliefs and prompt them to reconsider unfavourable beliefs. Students are very successful in hiding their thoughts and feelings, leading to misconceptions about their values, self-efficacy beliefs and outcome expectations.

The set of principles addressed in this booklet will hopefully provide more insight into students' motivational beliefs and into the way these beliefs affect their involvement, commitment and engagement in the life classroom. Knowledge of these principles will, I hope, act as guidelines for helping students to establish favourable motivational beliefs and unmask unfavourable beliefs.

Unfavourable Motivational Beliefs Impede Learning

Students are not motivated to learn in the face of failure.

Research Findings

Fear of failure does not automatically lead to passivity or avoidance. What matters are the motivational beliefs that have been attached to a subject-matter area. For example, Stefano has dominantly favourable beliefs about mathematics and unfavourable beliefs in relation to language learning. Domain-specificity of motivational beliefs implies that a student may be failure-oriented in some domains and not in others. Stefano no longer perceives a relationship between what he can do (his actions) and the outcomes of his actions (success or failure) in the language domain. He feels uncertain, stating that he is unable to perform the tasks well. Students give different reasons for their success or failure in various school subjects and these reasons are consistent with their self-concept of ability in that domain. The main reasons Stefano gives for his poor performance in languages in his lack of ability. Other frequently used excuses for poor performance are lack of effort (Sandra: 'I did poorly in history today because I did not put in a lot of effort'), bad luck (Stefano: 'I was unlucky that I was called upon first to consider that question'), inadequate strategy use (Stefano: 'I solved that math problem correctly, but I did not know that we had to write down the solution steps as well') and task characteristics (Sandra: 'The math problem was just to difficult'). Children who view poor performance as the result of low ability expect failure to occur again and again. These students experience negative thoughts and feelings (*e.g.* Sandra: 'I am the only one with seven mistakes. The teacher will not like me because I am a dumb kid'). Negative thoughts that are repeatedly associated with a task or activity become attached to similar learning situations. As such, a whole domain may be categorized as 'too difficult' or 'threatening'. Once these unfavourable motivational beliefs have become part of a student's theory of self, they will be activated again and again, creating doubt and anxiety. Unfavourable beliefs impede the learning process because they direct the learners' attention away from the learning activity itself, focusing it instead on their low ability. Even though children's understanding of causality changes with age, their beliefs about the cause of their successes and failures in a particular domain are very resistant to change.

Motivating Your Students

Students who state that they will never be able to complete the task successfully signal to you that they no longer perceive a link between their actions and a positive outcome. You can help them to re-establish the link by creating learning situations where they can experience success. However, it is not sufficient that they get the correct solution. They also need to understand why the solution plan was correct and what they can do (actions) to improve their skill further. Your students' attention has to be drawn explicitly to the link between their actions and the outcome of their actions by asking questions such as: 'What did you do to get the solutions? How do you know that the strategy you used is effective? Would this strategy work for the following problem as well? Why or why not?'

Paradoxically, students who have established unfavourable motivational beliefs are not interested in such process-oriented feedback. They only want to know whether their answer is correct, or whether they are on the right track. Try to be alert when your students request outcome-related feedback. Focus on what they have already mastered (*e.g.* 'Stefano, you got three correct. That is better than yesterday.') rather than on their shortcomings. Better still, point out the strengths of their solution plan. Such process-oriented feedback gives them a feeling of progress, which is necessary to build up a positive identity as a successful learner. Gradually stimulate them to reflect on their own performance (self-assessment). For example, encourage Stefano to verbalize why the corrected sentence conveys his message better.

Favourable Motivational Beliefs Facilitate Learning

Students who value the learning activity are less dependent on encouragement, incentives and reward.

Research Findings

Students are more interested in doing activities for which they think they have the necessary competence, or that they value (*e.g.* Stefano: 'I like math because it is easy, and I need it to become a space engineer', or Sandra: 'I don't like math, but I do my best because my dad tells me that it is important'). Students who value new skills have established favourable motivational beliefs. The chances are good that they are interested in opportunities to practice these skills. It is important to distinguish such commitment from mere compliance with the teacher-set goals. Many students complete tasks that they do not value all that much simply because they expect some sort of reward (*e.g.* high marks, a pass, or social approval). Students who undertake learning tasks purely for the sake of getting a reward from others, or in order to avoid some penalty, are extrinsically motivated (*e.g.* Stefano: 'I hate grammar exercises, but my mother prepares my favourite meal when I have to study for a test'). An activity is generally considered to be intrinsically motivating if external reward is not necessary for students to initiate and continue that activity. Favourable motivational beliefs are attached to the activity itself. Students who are intrinsically motivated will report that they do not have to invest effort and that doing the activity is gratifying (*e.g.* Sandra: 'when I am writing poetry or stories for the school bulletin, I lose track of time'). When difficulties arise, these students will persist with the activity because they experience a feeling of self-determination.

Motivating Your Students

Unfortunately, not all students are intrinsically motivated and you also have to cater to those students who are less motivated to learn. It is important to realize that classroom climate and the way interact with your students facilitates or impedes their motivation. Try to make tasks and activities meaningful for your students by referring to the intrinsic value of the task and to potential applications in other subject areas and outside school. How can you help your students to develop favourable motivational beliefs? Translate the curriculum in terms of the skills that your students find relevant and interesting. Find out what their current interests and future career goals are (*e.g.*,

Sandra wants to become a nurse and Stefano wants to become a space engineer). Show a video, a newspaper cutting, or tell a story, highlighting the importance and functional relevance of new content and skills. Ask students who are already motivated to explain why they value these new skills. Alternatively, ask your students to interview their parents, other teachers in school or older students to find out when they use the new content or skills. These activities will catch your students' attention and curiosity. This is already half of the motivation story. The other half is holding their interest. It is important that students perceive an optimal match between perceived demands and their current capacity. Allow them to adapt exercises according to their current capacity. For example, Stefano gets bored when math problems are too easy. Do not force him to cover the content of the lesson at the same pace, or in the same way, as the slower learners. Also, encourage students who find a math problem too demanding, to redesign it in such a way that it becomes less threatening (*e.g.* Sandra: 'Can I do this math problem together with Claudia?). Allowing students to adopt a learning activity to their own psychological needs gives them a feeling of autonomy and self-determination. Denying them this right will be interpreted as external pressure to comply.

Students' Beliefs About Goal Orientation

Students who are mastery-oriented learn more than students who are ego-oriented.

Research Findings

As important motivational belief that has not been discussed so far is goal orientation. The way students' orient themselves to learning tasks within a domain is a strong indicator of their engagement and performance. Students who learn because they want to master a new skill use more effective learning strategies than students who are ego-oriented. The latter students engage in learning tasks with the intention to demonstrate success (approach ego-orientation) or to hide failure (avoidance ego-orientation). The motivation process of mastery-oriented students differs from that of ego-oriented students in many ways. For example, Stefano shows mastery-orientation in relation to the math domain and ego-orientation in relation to language domain.

He starts on his math home-work before dinner because he wants to find out whether he can solve the problems. He is prepared to invest effort because he values mathematics and enjoys improving his math skills. When Stefano meets obstacles while doing math, he asks himself: 'How can I make it work?' He is not ashamed that others hear about his mistakes. On the contrary, he always volunteers to show his solution plan, because he appreciates the feedback he gets. In contrast, Stefano does not want others to find out that he made many spelling and grammatical mistakes in a text.

Sandra also values mathematics but for different reasons. She is ego-oriented in math class. She wants to demonstrate success to change others people's opinion about her math ability. Sandra invests effort in math as long as she feels confident that she can find the correct solution. She gives up when she spots mistakes, because she believes that there is only one correct solution. These beliefs fuel her fear that others will use her mistakes as proof of her math ability.

Two research findings should be reported here. Firstly, students display a dominant goal orientation (ego or mastery) by the time they are in second grade, and striving for ego-orientation goals becomes more dominant as children proceed through primary school. They become progressively more concerned with their self-worth, express more concern for peer-status and avoid doing things that the group rejects (fear of alienation). By the fourth grade, avoidance ego goals (*e.g.* wanting to hide mistakes) have already assumed a prominent position. A second finding shows that teachers set up dominantly competitive or co-operative learning settings in class. Teachers who highlight evaluation procedures, give public feedback, frequently make social comparisons and refer to individual abilities create a competitive atmosphere and elicit ego-oriented thoughts and feelings.

Motivating Your Students

The extent to which you succeed in creating a mastery-oriented learning setting is an indication of your professional competence. You can play down ego-orientation by explaining to your students that you are not interested in seeing one correct outcome, but that you focus instead on their attempts to come up with a solution strategy. Students will only believe this 'trying is more important than the product' statement when you act according to what you preach. In other words, provide feed-back with respect to the solution plan, encourage students to exchange information about the strategies they used and allow them to learn from their mistakes. This is a difficult job since ego-oriented students get annoyed when they have to reflect on their mistakes. By using supportive comments that highlight their involvement progress and effort you will convince them that you value their attempts to solve problems, particularly when they reflect about what did not work out and why. Mastery-orientation will develop when these students take pride in finding parts of a solution and in catching errors in progress.

Different Beliefs About Effort Affect Learning Intentions

Students expect value for effort.

Research Findings

Students decide how much effort they will allocate to a learning task on the basis of their self-concept of ability and their effort beliefs. Young children are notorious over-estimators or under-estimators of their own performance. They may rate themselves among the best of their class, even though their performance is absolutely below the mark. Young children have a rather naïve theory of effort. They believe that if they want something badly enough and do their best to accomplish it, they will be valued for their effort. In other words, they think they have control over the learning situation and keep their high expectations of success even after repeated failure. Their conceptualization of effort as the most important explanation of their successes and failures is a strong motivator to keep practising.

However, as students get older, the messages they receive from parents and teachers change gradually. More emphasis is put on their ability as a major source of success and failure than on their effort. Children learn to take into account their actual experiences and evaluative feedback from others. They also engage in social comparisons with their peers. This implies that their domain-specific self-efficacy beliefs become more accurate and realistic. Simultaneously, they link these beliefs to their emerging theory of effort. By the age of 9, children seem to have lost confidence in effort as the overall source of success. Research evidence is clear: domain-specific self-efficacy beliefs influence effort investment, and not the other way round. Students like Stefano, who believe that they are good in mathematics, are willing to invest effort to acquire math skills, but they do not necessarily invest more observable effort. Their task-engagement is fundamentally different from that of students who believe they lack efficiency. More specifically, these students use adequate cognitive strategies that lead to good results. Students like Sandra, who believe that their math skills are deficient, may also invest effort in mathematics. However, they do a lot of things that are ineffective, such as sitting and sighing in front of their books, copying a lot of exercises, rereading several pages. This type of effort creates anxiety and frustration and leads to poor performance. Research has shown that teachers can coach students to develop their effort beliefs. Interestingly, teachers who coach effort are rewarded by enhanced intrinsic motivation.

Motivating Your Students

Teacher observations confirm that students develop a threshold for declaring whether or not they have put in sufficient effort to reach the learning goal. They use specific stop rules. For example, Sandra may say: 'I have worked for more than an hour now. This must be sufficient for my math homework', or 'I have worked harder for mathematics than for history'. Stefano may justify thus: 'I don't have to work hard for math, I just do the exercises and it usually works out well', or 'I have worked longer than any of my friends to write a good text—this must be sufficient'.

In general, students' theory of effort is underdeveloped. They need assignments to build up domain-specific effort beliefs and to be encouraged to update these beliefs as their skills develops. When you encourage and value effort, your students will begin to view themselves as responsible for their own learning. It is essential, however, that you provide your students with adequate feedback. A good way to start is by providing assignments that require students to predict the effort needed to do a task. After finishing the task, students could be asked to reflect on the invested effort. Was it sufficient or superfluous, and why? Once students get into the habit of reflecting on their effort, they are better equipped to self-regulate their own learning.

GOAL SETTING AND APPRAISAL

Students need encouragement and feedback on how to develop motivational strategies.

Research Findings

Students who define teacher-set goals in terms of their own reasons for learning create a commitment to a desire end-state. Their goal-setting process differs fundamentally from that of students who merely comply with the teacher's expectations. Recent findings indicate that learning goals that are agreed upon jointly by the students and the teacher have a better chance of being accomplished. Such an agreement reflects the intention of both parties to invest effort.

Setting a learning goal refers to the selection of a motivation strategy that fits the actual learning situation. This strategy consists of active attempts on the part of the learner to activate favourable motivational beliefs, to pay attention to relevant cues in the learning environment, and to ignore cues that are distracting from learning. Students who take the time to appraise learning situations in terms of their own goals discover desirable and undesirable end-states. For example, Stefano hated all exercises in which he had to use a dictionary. However, recognition of desirable outcomes of a language activity was a turning point in his attitude. His teacher recommended that he send a letter to a Scottish boy who wants to become a space engineer. Stefano's favourable appraisal of the pen-pal context and the anticipated desirable outcomes (getting an answer) turned him from a passive language learner into an active one. He learned to pay attention to positive outcomes and ignore undesired end-states (spelling mistakes), and he discovered the power of writing as a tool for communication.

Students who begin the learning process by activating favourable beliefs, particularly mastery-orientation and self-efficacy beliefs, need less encouragement from others to get started. Moreover, favourable motivational beliefs draw students' attention to cues in the environment that elicit further interest and confidence in their own capacity to do the task.

Motivating Your Students

Within the context of the classroom, the teachers' main goal is to get through the syllabus. Most teachers still overrate their students' capacity to set their own learning goals. Hardly any time or effort is devoted to obtaining the students' opinions about the relevance and value of the learning tasks. Consequently, students can motivate themselves for out-of-class activities but do not have a clue about how they can motivate themselves for their schoolwork. Yet, in the goal-setting phase, students lay the foundation for further learning and for the development of interest. What can be done to encourage your students to develop motivation strategies? The goal-setting process can be facilitated by asking students to stop and think about why a particular learning task is important, relevant, fun, boring, challenging, difficult or easy. Why are they confident (or doubtful) about their own skills to do a task, and what triggers their doubt or confidence? When students have completed a task they can reflect on their original appraisal of the task again. Ask them to formulate in their own words whether their appraisal of the task has changed and why. By asking your students to reflect on their initial competence and relevance judgements in relation to different learning tasks and about their initial outcome expectations, you create a favourable classroom climate for goal setting. Your students will feel free to make their appraisals explicit and open for discussion, raise questions about their own and other students' motivation for learning, and learn from each other. If you show interest in the reasons why your students consider some topics as their favourites while others find these topics boring, both you and your students will gain information about what makes motivation strategies work.

Striving for Goals and Willpower

Students need encouragement and feedback on how to develop willpower.

Research Findings

Good intentions that were strong in the goal-setting stage do not automatically lead to goal accomplishment. Many learning goals need active striving on the part of the learner in order to be accomplished, meaning that effort needs to be invested. Efforts refers to an intentional act that increases commitment to a task, such as increasing attention, concentration and the amount of time spent on a task, or by doing specific activities (*e.g.* re-reading, rehearsal, underlining, paraphrasing, copying). However, effort often declines when a task gets more complex or less interesting, when obstacles are encountered, or when students are distracted by competing activities. At such a point, they need willpower to sustain attention and effort.

Parents and teachers alike view persistence as an important aspects of willpower. Yet, research has shown that persistence is not necessarily a virtue. Some students try the same strategy again and again in order to complete a task (high persistence) while others discard a strategy at the first sign of failure (low persistence). Results from recent studies suggest that two important learning strategies should be implemented. The first strategy deals with the students' capacity to initiate a solution plan without too much hesitation. The second strategy deals with the students' capacity to judge whether it is fruitful to continue with a solution plan (persistence), or whether it is better to give it up because it will lead nowhere (disengagement).

Before initiating a learning activity, students should orient themselves to the learning task in terms of its purpose and possible solution plans. Effective decisions to persist in the goal-striving stage are based on this knowledge. Students who have a good conception of the learning goal and also have access to a repertoire of strategies to generate an adequate solution plan use their effort constructively. They can judge which strategies are useful and also monitor whether the selected strategies are effective to reach the goal. If they notice that a chosen strategy is not effective, they can select a new one and test whether it is more effective or else disengage from the task because they judge that effort is no longer fruitful (*e.g.* not enough time or resources). Students who have a misconception of the goal or lack adequate strategies may also persist, but their effort is largely undirected. For example, Sandra often tries several solution plans blindly when she is doing her math homework in the hope that one will work.

Motivating Your Students

How can you help your students to develop willpower? First of all, you should not be misled by observed effort. When effort investment is high (or low), you still need to know why that is the case. In order to be able to interpret student initiative, persistence and disagreement meaningfully, you need to have a good idea of the way your students perceive the learning goal and also of how much effort they need to invest to reach it. Students should be given plenty of opportunities to practice striving for goals. You can coach this process by reminding them to set a series of sub-goals and to compose a checklist that will help them to monitor, assess and reflect on the quality of their engagement and commitment during the solution process.

Reflecting on the goal-striving process implies that students should raise questions about the resources that are necessary and sufficient to reach various sub-goals. For example, Stefano may ask himself: Do I have sufficient time to finish my history homework before dinner if I reread every section twice and make a brief summary? Post-activity reflection about effort investment is essential to make students aware of their attempts at effort management and of the reason why they did not exercise willpower. By asking your students to compare and contrast the amount and type of effort invested in various tasks, you can help them to develop their theory of effort, and at the same time allow them to gain insight into their own willpower.

Keeping Multiple Goals in Harmony

Students are more committed to learning if the objectives are compatible with their own goals.

Research Findings

Teachers, educators and parents are convinced that acquiring new knowledge and skills is the most important goal that students should strive for in a school context. The reality is different. Youngsters do not consider the learning goals set by the teacher as the most salient goals in their life. They pursue many other goals as well. For example, they want to be treated fairly, build up a network of friends, learn more about their favourite topics and discuss romantic partners. These personal goals play a crucial role in motivation processes by defining their content, direction and intensity. Recent evidence suggests that students are more motivated towards their schoolwork when school-related goals are in harmony with their own wishes, needs and expectations. For instance, Sandra adores her teacher and uses her as a role model because she acknowledges that Sandra wants to become a nurse and frequently relates schoolwork to this important goal. Students who note that the teacher acknowledges their personal goals accept the teacher's goals more easily. By contrast, students who realize that their personal goals are ignored, or even thwarted, rebel against the system and consider the curriculum as alien to their 'real' life.

Teachers and parents often complain that students do not adopt the goals they hold for them, and that they do not follow up on their well-meant advice. For example, Stefano's father tries to prevent him from doing his homework with the radio on, believing that music affects motivation and performance negatively. Current research does not support this view. Yet, such conflicts of interest lead to the frustration of Stefano's need for autonomy. Often, teachers (and parents) try to push their own goals along, thus fuelling the child's struggle for autonomy. For decades, schools, teachers and researchers narrowed educational goals to learning and achievement, which only frustrated students' social goals.

Motivating Your Students

Students bring their own goals into the classroom and want to negotiate with you about how, when, and with whom they want to reach the learning goals. It is important to realize that you impose many goals on your students, including social goals (*e.g.* 'You have to work individually, without the support or help from your peers'; or 'You have to work in small groups and take responsibility for the learning of members of your group'). Peers also impose goals on other students (*e.g.* 'Ignore the teacher when he asks for volunteers'). When students realize that their own goals are discordant with your goals, they make attempts to align the curricular goals with their own goals. For example, Sandra may ask: 'Can I hand in my homework tomorrow because I did not have enough resource material to make a good job of it?' Similarly, Stefano may request: 'Can I do this task alone, because I have a different opinion than the rest of my group?' If you grant these requests, your students will experience self-determination. The positive cognitions and feelings that are part of that experience will further the learning process On the contrary, if you deny these requests, they will experience a conflict of goals and may not take responsibility for achieving the curricular goals. Many forms of misbehaviour in class can be interpreted in terms of a goal conflict. You will deal more flexibly with misbehaviour when you view it as a signal that a salient goal is being frustrated. For example, Stefano may say: 'How can I work efficiently on a math problem if you want me to help students who always run into problems?' Likewise, Sandra may ask: 'Why can't we do this task together?' It is important to realize that your students want to be treated with respect. They expect you to explain why you turn down their requests.

Conclusion

It is often stated that bad teaching kills motivation and that good teaching brings out the best in students of all ages. If you want to encourage your students to become their own teachers and develop independent learning skills, you need to know about the principles that guide motivated learning. The eight principles that are addressed in this booklet apply to children and adolescents from different countries and different cultures. I described the principles in such a way that you gain insight into the reasons why students are or are not motivated to learn in the context of the classroom. However, you still need to adapt these principles to the local context of your classroom. I focused on two primary school students, Stefano and Sandra, and referred to their thinking and feeling in relation to the mathematics an language domains, yet the principles do not refer to particular curricula or specific age groups. Rather, they refer to generic aspects of motivated learning that cut across school subjects, grade levels and types of education. They focus on the students' beliefs, opinions and values and how these motivational beliefs affect learning. Knowledge of your students' motivational beliefs will help you to create learning environments that are well suited to their psychological needs. The capacity to listen to your students and observe their behaviour in the live classroom will help to inform you of what they find interesting, challenging, boring and threatening, and why they have this opinion. Willingness to negotiate with your students and grant them autonomy will convince them that you are truly interested in how and why they learn. A good way to start your observations is by selecting one or more students in your class who think, feel and behave somewhat like Stefano or Sandra. Observe these students in the next few weeks and discover how the eight motivational principles that are described in this booklet work in *your* classroom.

REFERENCES

Boekaerts, M. 1997. Self-regulated Learning: A New Concept Embraced by Researchers, Policy Makers, Educators, Teachers, and Students, *Learning and Instruction* (Tarrytown, NY), Vol. 7, No. 2, p. 151-86.

—. 1998. Boosting Students' Capacity to Promote their Own Learning: A Goal Theory Perspective. *Research Dialogue in Learning and Instruction* (Exeter, UK), Vol. 1, No. 1, p. 13-22.

—.1999. Coping in Context: Goal Frustration and Goal Ambivalence in Relation to Academic and Interpersonal goals. *In*: Frydenberg, E. ed. *Learning to Cope: Developing As a Person in Complex Societies*, p. 175-97. Oxford, UK, Oxford University Press.

—. 2001. Pro-active Coping: Meeting Challenges and Achieving Goals. *In*: Frydenberg, E., ed. *Beyond Coping: Meeting Goals, Visions and Challenges*. Oxford, UK, Oxford University Press.

Burning, R.; Horn, C. 2000. Developing Motivation to Write. *Educational Psychologist* (Hillsdale, NJ), Vol. 35, No. 1, p. 25-37.

Corno, L.; Randi, J. 1997. Motivation, Violation and Collaborative Innovation in Classroom Literacy, *In*: Guthrie, J.; Wigfield, A., eds. *Reading, Engagement: Motivating Readers Through Integrated Instruction*, p. 14-31. Newark, DE, International Reading Association.

Covington, M.V. 1992. *Making the Grade: A Self-Worth Perspective on Motivation and School Reform*. Cambridge, UK; New York, Cambridge University Press.

Elliot, A.J. 1999. Approach and Avoidance Motivation and Achievement Goals. *Educational Psychologist* (Mahwah, NJ), Vol. 34, No. 3, p. 169-89.

Guthrie, J.T.; Solomon, A. 1997. Designing Contexts to Increase Motivations for Reading. *Educational Psychologist* (Mahwah, NJ), Vol. 32, No. 2, p. 95-103.

Maehr, M.L. 1984. Meaning and Motivation: Toward a Theory of Personal Investment. *In*: Ames, R.E.; Ames, C., eds. *Research on Motivation in Education: Vol. 1. Student Motivation*, p. 115-44. San Diego, CA, Academic Press.

Niemivirta, M. 1999. Motivational and Cognitive Predictors of Goal Setting and Task Performance. *International Journal of Educational Research* (Oxford, UK), Vol. 31, p. 499-513.

Pintrich, P.R. 2001. The Role of Goal Orientation in Self-Regulated Learning. *In:* Boekaerts, M.; Pintrich, P.R. Zeidner, M. eds. *Handbook of Self-Regulation*, p. 451-502. San Diego, CA, Academic Press.

Ryan, R.M.; Deci, E.L. 2000. Self-Determination Theory and the Facilitation of Intrinsic Motivation, Social Development, and Well-Being. *American Psychologist* (Washington, DC), Vol. 55, p. 68-78.

Ryan, A.M.; Gheen, M.H.; Midgley, C. 1998. Why Some Students Avoid Asking for Help: An Examination of the Interplay Among Students' Academic Efficacy, Teachers' Social-Emotional Role, and the Classroom Goal Structure. *Journal of Educational Psychology* (Washington, DC), Vol. 90, No. 3, p. 528-35.

Skinner, E.A. 1995. *Perceived Control, Motivation and Coping*. Thousand Oaks, CA, Sage Publications.

Stipek, D.J. 1988. *Motivation to Learn: From Theory to Practice*. Englewood Cliffs, NJ, Prentice Hall.

Turner, J.C.; Meyer, D.K. 1998. Integrating Classroom Context into Motivation Theory and Research: Rationales, Methods and Implications. *In*: Urdan, T.; Maehr, M.; Pintrich, P., eds. *Advances in Motivation and Achievement: A Research Annual, Vol. 11*, p. 87-121. Greenwich, CT, JAI Press.

Vermeer, H.; Boekaerts, M.; Seegers, G. 2000. Motivational and Gender Differences: Sixth-grade Students' Mathematical and Problem-Solving Behaviour. *Journal of Educational Psychology* (Washington, DC), Vol. 92, No. 2, p. 308-15.

Wentzel, K.R. 1996. Social and Academic Motivation in Middle School: Concurrent and Long-Term Relations to Academic Effort. *Journal of Early Adolescence* (Thousand Oaks, CA), Vol. 16, No. 4, p. 390-406.

Wlodkowski, R.J.; Jaynes, J.H. 1990. *Eager to Learn*. San Francisco, CA, Jossey Bass Publishers

Courtesy: International Bureau of Education and International Academy of Education.

7

Preventing Behaviour Problems: *What Works?*

*Sharon L. Foster**
*Patricia Brennan***
*Anthony Biglan****
*Linna Wang*****
*Saud Al-Ghaith******

Introduction

Many societies consider delinquency, violence, drug and alcohol abuse, smoking, and early pattern of sexual behaviour that risk sexually transmitted diseases and pregnancy among never married teenagers to be serious problems. These problems can ruin adolescents' lives by leading them to be put in jail, by limiting their education and vocational training opportunities, by having unwanted children, and by risking the development of serious illnesses. In addition, these problems are costly to a society in economic terms. Crime, drug and alcohol abuse,

* Alliant International University in San Diego, California, USA.

** Emory University, Georgia, USA.

*** Oregon Research Institute Oregon, USA.

**** Alliant International University, California, USA.

***** Saudi Arabia.

smoking and high-risk sexual behaviour result in huge health care, judicial and victim-related costs over the life span of an adolescent with serious behaviour problems.

Adolescents who display serious problems in one of these areas frequently develop problems in other areas, too. Many studies from various countries indicate that delinquency, smoking, drug and alcohol use, and sexual behaviour that can cause disease are strongly correlated with each other. All of these problems are also associated with academic failure and school dropout. Furthermore, adolescents with more than one of these problems are particularly likely to experience many of the serious and costly consequences of teen violence, drug and alcohol misuse, and risky sexual behaviour. This makes it particularly important to prevent the development of serious behaviour problems.

Research indicates that many of the same factors contribute to the development of all of these problems in adolescence. This suggests that early intervention to reduce these risk factors may prevent a whole range of problems. For some societies, there are new problems and they may require new approaches to prevent them. Fortunately, evidence suggests that interventions—particularly interventions that occur when children are young—that address risk factors for these behaviours can reduce the chances that children will develop these serious behaviour problems as they reach adolescence. These risk factors and interventions have several common features. We describe these common features in the principles of effective prevention included in this chapter.

Start Prevention Early

Prevention efforts should begin with prenatal care and continue throughout the school years.

Research Findings

Risk factors for behaviour problems occur throughout children's development, and children face new risks as they mature and encounter new challenges. Children's environments also become more complex as they grow older, making intervention more difficult. Some early risks have been repeatedly tied to many behaviour problems in later childhood. Reducing these risks has the possibility to prevent the development of multiple problems.

A few programmes have had remarkable effects in preventing the development of problem behaviour in adolescence. In one project, nurses visited poor unmarried teenage mothers before and after, the birth of their children. Their visits focused on improving the mother's physical and psychological health, educational and family planning, childcare and support from family and friends. The mother's own adjustment improved. More importantly, their children showed less delinquency, smoking, drug and alcohol use and sexual activities at age 15, compared to children whose mothers did not receive the programme.

School interventions that begin when children enter school have had similar effects. These approaches typically taught teachers to apply systematic consequences for desirable and undesirable behaviour. Children learned skills for thinking through problem situations and for interacting in co-operative, non-aggressive ways with peers. Some school interventions involved parents by teaching them ways to interact positively with their children and to discipline misbehaviour effectively.

Other effective approaches begin as children enter adolescence. These often provide information on drug and alcohol use and abuse. They provide messages to counteract stereotypes in films, magazines, and movies that using alcohol, tobacco, and drugs in glamorous. Children also practice specific ways to refuse peer invitations to use drugs or alcohol.

Interventions do not work equally well. Some project that involve nurses to help mothers before and after the birth of a child (like the one just described) have been very successful. Others have not. The specific goals and services involved in these programmes are important. Furthermore, staff members must be trained and put services into practice in ways that follow the methods that produced proven positive results. Programme quality matters, both in what goes into the programme and in how people deliver the programme.

In Schools and Communities

- Early interventions should address prenatal care and social and economic adjustment of mothers after a child is born.
- Mothers who are young, poor and never married may particularly benefit from prevention programmes. Their children are less likely to have problems as they grow up, resulting in fewer costs to their societies.
- Schools provide important places to offer preventive interventions. Times when children enter new school environments—such as when they first attend school, encounter new academic demands, or move from smaller to larger schools—are particularly good times for intervention.
- Schools and communities should select culturally appropriate programmes carefully based on evidence that the approach reduces children's behaviour problems. Teachers and other adults should follow the guidelines for these programmes. Too much modification may cause a programme to lose its effectiveness.

Positive Consequences Matter

Provide positive consequences to increase desirable behaviours.

Research Findings

One of the best-established principles of learning is that appropriate, immediate positive consequences can make behaviour more frequent. This process is commonly called positive reinforcement. Similarly, increasing positive incentives for alternatives to problem behaviour can lead to decreases in problem behaviour. At the societal level, economists' work clearly shows that changing incentives that involve money produces changes in business and societal practices. When adults provide positive consequences for a child's co-operative behaviour, non-violent ways of handling conflict, and involvement with peers who are involved in desirable activities, they steer youth away from problem behaviour. Furthermore, most of the effective prevention programmes that begin when children enter school or that work with parents of aggressive children teach adults to use positive consequences systematically. By doing this, adults encourage, children to develop in positive ways.

Positive incentives come in many forms and can be tangible (such as money) or social (for example, praise). Additional examples of positive consequences that can increase behaviour involve giving children extra privileges and opportunities that they desire. Other consequences, such as attention from others, can be more subtle but equally powerful. Parents, teachers, other adults or peers can provide positive consequences to children. Similarly, adults and children can provide positive consequences that can help adults display more positive behaviour.

Positive consequences can also inadvertently encourage problem behaviour. A teen who can earn needed money by selling drugs may sell or use drugs; a boy who routinely gains attention from his peers for breaking the law may continue this criminal behaviour.

In Schools and Communities

- Teachers should provide positive consequences for positive social as well as academic accomplishments, particularly with children and youth that misbehave frequently.
- Consequences can come in many forms: positive attention, praise, privileges, access to desirable activities, prizes and money all act as positive consequences. Children showing problem behaviour may need more frequent, immediate and salient positive consequences to improve their behaviour than children with fewer problems. All children, however, can benefit from knowing when they have done a good job, either academically or socially.
- Teachers with large numbers of children who misbehave should examine whether adults or other children are unknowingly providing positive consequences—particularly attention—for the behaviour

they want to discourage. Rearranging the environment so that children get attention, privileges, etc., for more positive social academic beahviour can help this situation.

- Many programmes help teach parents and teachers to use consequences effectively. Schools can offer these programmes to help adults learn to help children develop in more pro-social ways.
- Adults need positive consequences, too. Decision-makers should support, praise and acknowledge school administrators' and teachers' effective use of the kinds of principles that make a difference in preventing and reducing child and adolescent behaviour problems.

Effective Negative Consequences Matter

Clear, immediate, mild negative consequences can reduce problem behaviours.

Research Findings

Just as positive consequences can increase the chances a behaviour will occur, effective negative consequences will reduce its probability. Negative consequences, like positive consequences, can be tangible or social. Behaviour often decreases when that behaviour 'costs' the person something in time, money or undesirable consequences.

One clear set of costs that affect problem behaviour involves financial costs. Individuals who pay fines for criminal offences are less likely to re-offend in the future, especially when the fine is proportional to the offender's ability to pay. When the cost of smoking or alcohol goes up, adolescent substance use goes down. Social 'costs' of problem behaviour can include loss of privileges or a mild reprimand in which the adult tells the child briefly what he or she did wrong and why it is a problem. Another negative consequence that works well for some children involves briefly removing them from the ongoing activity for about five minutes and asking them to sit quietly by themselves in an isolated place. Adults typically think of these consequences as 'punishment'. Severe negative consequences that cause physical or emotional harm to children are generally called 'abuse' and should not be used.

Unfortunately, many of the ways that adults try to punish problem behaviours do not work in the long run to reduce problems even if they get someone to stop a negative behaviour for the moment. In particular, parents of children with behaviour problems often spend a great deal of time disciplining their children with methods that are highly negative but do not work. Putting youth in jail—another common punishment for youth crime—also generally fails to prevent youth from committing future crimes after they leave jail. Many effective programmes for preventing serious adolescent behaviour problems teach parents and teachers to discipline problem behaviour in new, non-abusive, more effective ways.

The reason punishment often fails to work is probably because the punishment is too severe, too delayed and too inconsistent. Costs and other negative consequences will work best if: *(a)* negative consequences or costs occur immediately after the behaviour; *(b)* negative consequences are consistent rather than occasional; and *(c)* the child receives positive consequences for desirable alternative behaviours. Gradually increasing the intensity of punishment is not effective in the long run, either. Instead, relatively mild negative consequences delivered consistently are more likely to be effective—particularly when expectations for acceptable behaviour are clear.

In Schools and Communities

- Teachers should communicate classroom rules clearly so children understand which behaviours will result in negative consequences.
- Teachers and parents, should provide belief, immediate, mild and consistent negative consequences for problem behaviour. Examples include short, private reprimands that label the problem behaviour clearly; brief loss of privileges, or brief isolation from an activity the child enjoys.

- Teachers' negative consequences will work best if teachers also establish warm, positive relationships with their students and if they provide positive consequences for pro-social alternatives to problem behaviours.
- Teachers and adults should avoid negative consequences that have the potential to harm the child either physically or psychologically (*e.g.* insulting, children publicly).
- Teachers and other adults should carefully keep track of problems to see if their negative consequences decrease the frequency of problem behaviours. If not, they should try alternative ways of handling the child's behaviour.

BUILD SKILLS THROUGH PRACTICE

Create opportunities for children to observe and practice interpersonal as well as academic skills.

Research Findings

Two important factors that predict the development of anti-social behaviour and drug and alcohol use in adolescence are poor achievement in school and problems with peer relationships. These problems in turn are linked to poor academic and social skills. Although teachers typically focus on children's academic skills, they can also play important roles in helping children learn to interact appropriately with peers. Some of the most effective programmes for preventing drug, alcohol and tobacco use specifically teach adolescents how to resist peer pressure to become involved in problem behaviour. Effective prevention approaches that begin even earlier focus in part on teaching children to get along well with peers and to think through and resolve problem situations.

Children learn interpersonal skills in various ways. They observe parents, teachers and peers handle situations and learn from what they see. Adults also instruct children in how to behave. One thing is clear from research on teaching children to resist peers' encouragement to use tobacco, alcohol and drugs, however: adult instruction is not enough. Practising the skills is crucial, too. Children must also generalize what they have learned to real-life situations. Teaching children how to handle problem situations will be most effective if it involves: *(a)* instruction and opportunities to observe others behave effectively; *(b)* practise and feedback on the skills they are learning; *(c)* instruction in many different examples of the skills; and *(d)* positive consequences from adults or peers when children use their skills in their daily lives. In addition, children must learn skills that fit their culture and that will help them be more effective in the situations they encounter.

In Schools and Communities

- Teachers and parents should act in ways that show children how to handle problems well. Children imitate the behaviour of those who are important to them.
- Teach young children interpersonal skills for handling conflict non-violently and co-operating with others. Children can also benefit from learning cognitive skills for recognizing problem situations, stopping to think rather than responding impulsively, generating ways of solving problems, and evaluating the consequences of different solutions.
- Teach young adolescents specific ways for handling situations in which peers invite or pressure them to use drugs, tobacco, alcohol or to become involved in delinquency activities or risky sexual behaviour.
- Incorporate teaching interpersonal skills into classroom teaching. Make sure children have many opportunities to practise the skills they are learning and to receive feedback on how they are doing.
- Train children to use skills that are likely to be effective in real-life situations. Whenever possible, make sure that they receive positive consequences for using their skills. Children are likely to abandon what they have learned if they try a new behaviour and its fails to work for them.

- Children who have problems getting along with others are likely to have more difficulties than others with learning and mastering important interpersonal skills. They may need more practice and feedback than others and more systematic attempts to help them apply what they have learned.

MONITOR A CHILD'S BEHAVIOUR

Know where children and adolescents are, what they are doing and with whom, and provide appropriate supervision.

Research Findings

Adult knowledge of where children are and with whom they are interacting may help to prevent problem behaviour. When parents and teachers know what their children and students are doing, they can detect when the child is getting involved in activities that might pose a risk. Thus, they reduce opportunities for problems by steering their children away from risky situations. At the same time, they can provide positive reinforcement for desired behaviour and effective negative consequences when children violate rules or expectations.

Research indicates that young, adolescents are particularly likely to experiment with alcohol, tobacco and other drugs if they are at home or at a friend's house when there are no adults around. In schools, aggressive social behaviour is more likely where adult supervision is minimal, such as on the playground and in the hallways, than where adults are present. Similarly, delinquent activity is more likely to occur in the afternoon hours, when supervision is less likely, than earlier in the day. Furthermore, parents who know what their child to adolescent is doing each day are less likely to have children who associate with deviant peers and engage in diverse problem behaviours. Adolescents who have friends who break the law, smoke, drink or use illegal drugs are more likely to do these things than children whose friends are not involved in problem behaviours.

In Schools and Communities

- Encourage parents to ask where their children are, what they are doing and with whom using a non-interrogatory manner. These questions are especially important during the teenage years, when youth become more independent and spend more time away from home.
- A child should be gradually given increasing autonomy during adolescence. At the same time, adults should make informed choices in how much independence they grant and under what conditions.
- Encourage children to make friends with others who are not involved in problem behaviours.
- Avoid creating unsupervised groups of children with behaviour problems. Children may learn problem behaviour from each other and encourage each other to behave inappropriately. When these groups exist, monitor them closely to prevent youths from encouraging problem behaviour in their peers.
- Create enjoyable activities for children and teenagers that involve adult supervision. Supervised recreational activities allow children time to interact with peers but also keep children away from situations that may tempt them to try cigarettes, drugs, alcohol or risky sexual behaviour.
- Limit the amount of the time that children spend away from school and unsupervised during the day. Require students to stay or school grounds in supervised settings, and offer after-school programmes supervised by adults. Athletic activities, community service and—for older teenagers—employment also provide rewarding activities that involve adult supervision.

LIMIT OPPORTUNITIES FOR MISBEHAVIOUR

Reduce youths' access to the situations in which problem behaviour is particularly likely to occur.

Research Findings

Even the most troubled young people cannot engage in problem behaviours unless they have opportunities to do so. Limiting youths' access to tobacco, drugs and alcohol, and involvement in delinquent or violent behaviour is one important part of efforts to prevent problem behaviour among teenagers. Children can obtain cigarettes, alcohol, drugs and weapons from their friends or siblings as well as by buying or stealing them.

The child's community or neighbourhood also makes a difference in problem behaviour. Living in neighbourhoods in which alcohol and illegal substances are regularly available promotes greater substance use among youth. So does living in neighbourhoods in which children are exposed to high rates of violence.

Reducing access to cigarettes, drugs and alcohol reduces how often adolescents use these substances. Numerous studies show that car accidents among young people who have been drinking can be significantly reduced when laws and regulations make alcohol less available. These laws include increases in the legal drinking age in countries that permit alcohol consumption. Another way shown to decrease alcohol use involves increased enforcement or restrictions on sales of alcohol to children. Similar research on youth smoking indicates that communities that adopt and enforce laws that make sales of tobacco to young people illegal can significantly reduce how many adolescents use tobacco. Schools with policies that restrict smoking have lower smoking rates than those that lack these policies.

Consistently enforcing laws and rules is as important as creating them. Simply informing merchants about rules may not prevent illegal sales of Alcohol and tobacco to youth. Authorities should use more active methods such as testing whether clerks will sell tobacco to young people and rewarding merchants for refusing to sell to children and teenagers can reduce the availability of alcohol and tobacco.

In Schools and Communities

- Create clear rules in schools and laws in communities that prohibit supplying or selling tobacco, alcohol, illegal drugs or weapons to children and adolescents.

- Create clear school policies that state that the school does not permit students to use illegal substances or to engage in aggressive behaviour.
- Enforce rules that restrict supplying drugs, alcohol, tobacco and weapons to children.
- Make sure that children do not have access to drugs, alcohol, tobacco and weapons at home.
- Examine situations in which children and teenagers engage in problem behaviour and make specific plans to keep youth away from those situations. Provide attractive alternative activities for youth to take their place.

Reduce Environmental Stressors

Reduce children's exposure to negative conditions that cause stress.

Research Findings

Negative events and conditions that are stressful create difficulties for both parents and children. These difficulties in turn can increase the chances the child will develop later problems. For example, a mother's exposure to stress during pregnancy is related to behaviour problems in her child. These stressors can take many forms, such as maternal smoking or alcohol use during pregnancy, a difficult or prolonged delivery, or the experience of an influenza infection. The negative effect of these early life stressors can often be reversed by consistent and warm parenting practices after the baby is born.

Exposure to violence in the family and the community produces stress for children and adolescents. Repeated exposure to violence is believed to lead to changes in brain functioning, and has been related to increased risk for aggression and use of drugs and alcohol, particularly in boys. In addition, serious stress (such as divorce, unemployment and poverty) is associated with problems in parenting and family relationships. These parenting problems in turn can contribute to a child's behaviour problems.

Studies with animals and drug use suggest that a lack of control over environmental stress might lead to higher levels of substance abuse. It is believed that children are motivated to achieve control over their environment, and they will attempt to do so by regulating their body's exposure to stress and stimulation. During adolescence this attempt to control their environment may lead them to deliberately seek out chemical stimulation from street drugs like cocaine, or psychological stimulation from risky sexual behaviour and antisocial acts. Reducing the stress children and teens experience along with helping them deal with unavoidable stressful events may help prevent these negative outcomes.

In Schools and Communities

- Provide parent education classes on nutrition and smoking during pregnancy. Advise mothers concerning the potential benefits of a healthy pregnancy on the long-term academic and behavioural outcomes for their children.

- Train parents in warm, consistent child-rearing practices. Advice them about how these skills can help prevent the negative effects that can result if the child was exposed to stress earlier in life.

- Provide children with opportunities and pro-social skills that allow them some control over their environment especially during particularly stressful periods in their lives. Examples include opportunities to master new skills (*e.g.* in sports or the arts), to work with others on creative projects, and academic situations in which they can make choices for themselves.

- Teach children and adults ways of limiting the stress they experience and skills for dealing with stress that cannot be avoided.

- Provide parenting programmes and support for parents who experience divorce, unemployment and other stressful negative events that can disrupt their parenting skills.

LIMIT BIOLOGICAL RISKS

Encourage good biological functioning throughout development.

Research Findings

Genetic influences are not the only biological influences on a child's development. From the earliest stages of development, the biological influences that come from the child's brain and physiology can increase or decrease that their risk for behaviour problems. For example, maternal use of drugs and alcohol during pregnancy, children's head injuries and poor nutrition have all been linked to increased risk for child behaviour problems.

Fortunately, most non-genetic, biological risks have an environmental component that can be influenced through intervention. For example, exposure to lead and other toxins has been found to increase the risk for aggression. Exposure to such risks can be controlled by changing the child's home environment (eliminate the use of lead-based paints on the walls), or by educating parents and other caretakers about what products to keep out of the reach of children.

Biological and environmental risk factors tend to work together to produce negative effects on children's behaviour. Biological risk factors may not have negative effects in the context of a supportive and less stressful family environment. Similarly, environmental risk factors may have fewer negative effects when the child has been helped to maintain good biological functioning throughout development.

In School and Communities

- Provide safe environments for children to play and study in. Minimize exposure to harmful substances and other biological risk factors.
- Provide students with nutritious meals and with adequate medical care.
- Children who have been exposed to biological risks may need special attention. Parents and teachers should provide a warm supportive, and structured environment for their development.

Discourage Aggression

Reducing aggressive behaviour among young children can prevent many problems later on.

Research Findings

Children in pre-school and elementary school who are highly aggressive or uncooperative are likely to be rejected by their peers and do poorly in school. Many will not simply outgrow their aggressiveness. As they grow older, they are more likely than other children to use drugs and commit violent and non-violent crime. Aggressive children who are impulsive and have attention problems are particularly likely to continue to have problems as they grow up. Helping these children to become less aggressive can prevent many problems later.

Although aggressive behaviour is fairly stable, not all aggressive children will develop additional later problems. In addition, some children who are not aggressive when young will develop problems with substance use and delinquency when they reach adolescence. This is particularly true of girls, who are generally less physically aggressive than boys. Nonetheless, enough children with early aggression grow up to have later problems to make interventions with aggressive children an important step in preventing later problems. In addition, behaviour such as hitting, kicking, teasing, bullying and fighting need to be addressed because they cause problems in the daily lives of children, their classmates, their families and their teachers.

Many programmes have been shown to reduce aggression significantly among those who participate in them. Most are more effective when children are young (ages 4-8) than when children are older. Some of the most effective interventions with younger children also focus on non-compliance with adult commands, which often precedes the development of aggression. Others focus on children's behaviour in elementary schools, helping teachers to learn to apply effective consequences and to teach children skills for interacting with peers and solving problems in non-violent ways. Some of the best of these programmes involve both parents and teachers and help them to learn ways to deal with children's disruptive behaviour in the classroom and aggressive behaviour at home and at school.

In Schools and Communities

- Identify children who have problems with aggressive behaviour and make specific plans to reduce their aggression. Look for children who harm others by fighting, hitting, bullying, calling names or excluding peers.
- Use effective positive consequences to encourage children to behave co-operatively, follow classroom rules and use non-violent ways of resolving conflicts.
- Communicate clear rules that aggression is not permitted and use effective immediate negative consequences to respond to aggressive behaviour.
- Work with parents so that they learn effective ways of disciplining aggression and encouraging alternative behaviour at home.
- Offer parent and teacher-training programmes that teach effective ways of working with children to help them develop non-aggressive skills to reduce aggressive behaviour.
- Seek assistance from a qualified mental health professional for aggressive children who fail to respond to interventions based on the principles in this pamphlet. Aggressive children who are also rejected by peers, who act impulsively, who have problems paying attention in school and who have poor academic skills particularly need effective intervention.

CREATE APPROPRIATE NORMS

Establishing strong, clear norms for behaviour can influence youths' behaviour.

Research Findings

Norms refer to both how often a behaviour occurs in a group and the extent to which the group approves of the behaviour. Young people are more likely to engage in problem behaviours if they think that others do the same things or would approve if they engaged in it. Peer group norms are especially influential for problem behaviour, but family, school, neighbourhood and community norms are also important.

When young people believe that many of their peers use tobacco, alcohol and other drugs they are more likely to do so themselves. Young people generally over-estimate how many of their peers use drugs and, as a result, they may want to try them. Programmes to correct misperceptions about how much smoking and other drug use occurs can help prevent drug use. This has been shown in careful studies where some schools received information about how few young people actually use drugs, while other schools did not get such information. Many effective problems with adolescents also involve youth that participate in leadership roles in these programmes after training in how to implement their part of the programme.

The entertainment media, including cinema, television and music, also affect young people's perceptions of norms for behaviour. Evidence suggests that seeing aggressive behaviour on TV may make some children more aggressive. Some movies, television and music produced in the United States in particular may overemphasize undesirable behaviour. Parents can reduce the harmful effects of international and local media by keeping children from viewing or listening to programmes that present aggressive behaviour and other problem behaviour in a positive light. Schools can also reduce the harmful effects of aggressive media by teaching children that these shows are not accurate about the extent or results of violence and substance use.

In Schools and Communities

- Use school programmes and mass media messages to emphasize the positive things that young people are doing and to show that most young people are opposed to substance use and violent behaviour.
    - Limit the amount of time children spend viewing or listening to programmes that present aggressive behaviour and other problem behaviour in positive ways.
    - Schools can reduce the harmful effects of media by teaching children that television and films are not accurate about the extent or results of violence and substance use.

- Involve youth—particularly youth viewed positive by peers—in leadership roles in activities that discourage problem behaviour. This shows children that their peers do not value or approve of aggression, substance use or risky sexual behaviour.

Conclusion

Schools can play an important role in preventing problem behaviour, particularly when other parts of the community also become involved in prevention efforts. Many of the factors that increase a child's risk for developing behaviour problems affect their behaviour in school and their academic performance. Social and academic problems in school in turn make it even more likely that early problems will persist and become worse over time.

A number of approaches are useful for reducing aggressive behaviour and preventing later problems with delinquency, substance use and risky sexual behaviour. Many of these involve school programmes and teacher training as important components. Many also involve parents and community efforts to reduce youth problems and increase children's involvement in positive activities that will improve their skills and competencies. This booklet has described some of the key principles underlying the most effective of these programmes. Programmes using these principles will work best if leaders and organisations in the community work together, each doing what they can to prevent the development of serious problems.

REFERENCES

Biglan, A., et al. (In Preparation.) *Changing Destinies: Causes, Consequences, and Prevention of Multiple Behaviour Problems in Youth*. New York, NY, Guilford Press.

Brennan, P.; Grekin, E.; Mednick, S. 1999. Maternal Smoking during Pregnancy and Adult Male Criminal Outcomes. *Archives of General Psychiatry* (Chicago, IL), Vol. 56, p. 215-19.

Brennan, P.; Mednick, S. 1997. Perinatal and Medical Histories of Anti-Social Individuals. *In:* Stoff, D.; Breiling, J.; Maser, J., eds. *Handbook of Antisocial Behaviour*, p. 269-79. New York, NY, Wiley.

Brennan, P.; Raine, A. 1997. Biosocial Bases of Antisocial Behaviour: Psychophysiological, Neurological, and Cognitive Factors. *Clinical Psychology Review* (Kidlington, UK), Vol. 17, p. 589-604.

Brewer, D., et al. 1995. Preventing Serious, Violent, and Chronic Juvenile Offending: A Review of Evaluations of Selected Strategies in Childhood, Adolescence, and the Community. *In:* Howell, J., et al., eds. *Serious, Violent, and Chronic Juvenile Offenders: A Sourcebook*, p. 61-141. Thousand Oaks,. CA. Saga Publications.

Coie, J.; Miller-Johnson, S. 2001. Peer Factors and Interventions. *In:* Loeber, R:; Farrington, D., eds. *Serious and Violent Juvenile Offenders*, p. 191-210. Thousand Oaks, CA, Saga Publications.

Dishion, T.; McMahon, R. 1998. Parental Monitoring and the Prevention of Child and Adolescent Problem Behaviour: A Conceptual and Empirical Formulation. *Clinical Child and Family Psychology Review* (New York, NY), Vol. 1, p. 61-75.

Durlak, J.; Wells, A. 1997. Primary Prevention Mental Health Programmes for Children and Adolescents: A Meta-Analytic Review. *American Journal of Community Psychology* (New York, NY), Vol. 25, p. 115-52.

Elliott, S.; Gresham. F. 1993. Social Skills Interventions for Children. *Behaviour Modification* (Newbury Park, CA), Vol. 17, p. 287-313.

Forehand, R.; Long, N. 1996. *Parenting the Strong-Willed Child*. Chicago, Il, Contemporary Books, Inc.

Gottfredson, D. 2001. *Schools and Delinquency*. Cambridge, UK, Cambridge University Press.

Hansen, W. 1992. School-Based Substance Abuse Prevention: A Review of the State of the Art in Curriculum, 1980-1990. *Health Education* (Bradford, UK), Vol. 7, p. 403-30.

Jason, L.; Hanaway, L. 1997. *Remote Control: A Sensible Approach to Kids, TV, and the New Electronic Media*. Sarasota, FL, Professional Resource Press.

Olds, D.; Kitzman, H. 1993. Review of Research on Home Visiting for Pregnant Women and Parents of Young Children. *Failure of Children* (Los Altos, CA), Vol. 3 (3) , p. 53-92.

Olds, D., et al. 1998. Long-Term Effects of Nurse Home Visitation on Children's Criminal and Antisocial Behaviour: 15-year Follow-up of a Randomized Controlled Trial. *Journal of the American Medical Association* (Chicago, IL), Vol. 280, p. 1238-44.

Patterson, G.; Reid, J.; Dishion, T. 1992. *Antisocial Boys: A Social Interactional Approach*, Vol. 4, Eugene, OR, Castalia Publishing Company.

Peters, R.; McMahon, R., eds. 1996. *Preventing Childhood Disorders, Substance Abuse, and Delinquency*. Thousand Oaks, CA, Sage Publications, Inc.

Taylor, T.; Biglan, A. 1998. Behaviour Family Interventions for Improving Child Rearing: A Review of the Literature for Clinicians and Policy Makers. *Clinical Child and Family Psychology Review* (New York, NY), Vol. 1, p. 41-60.

Walker, H. 1995. *The Acting-Out Child: Coping with Classroom Disruption*. 2nd ed. Longmont, CO. Sopris West.

Walker, H.; Colvin, G.; Ramsey, E. 1995. *Antisocial Behaviour in School: Strategies and Best Practices*. Pacific Grove, CA, Brooks/Cole Publishing Co.

Webster-Stratton, C.; Taylor, T. 2001. Nipping Early Risk Factors in the Bud: Preventing Substance Abuse, Delinquency, and Violence in Adolescence Through Interventions Targeted at Young Children (0-8 years). *Prevention Science* (New York, NY), Vol. 2, p. 165-92.

Yehuda, R. 2000. Biology of Posttraumatic Stress Disorder. *Journal of Clinical Psychiatry* (New York, NY) Vol. 61, p. 14-21.

Courtesy: UNESCO's International Bureau of Education and International Academy of Education.

8

Wasted Opportunities When Schools Fail

Edward B. Fiske

Introduction

Leaders in the developing countries generally understand the importance of investing in basic education. They recognize that high levels of literacy and numeracy are prerequisites for creating a competitive workforce and a nation of effective parents and active citizens. But they also face an uphill battle in building education systems capable of providing basic education for all children, youth and adults. Financial and human resources are scarce, so difficult decisions must be made in determining how best to allocate them. Thus it is imperative that scarce resources be used as effectively as possible.

Unfortunately, this is not what is happening. Although significant progress has been made in increasing the number of pupils enrolled in school in developing countries, these gains are undermined by persistently large number of pupils who take more than one year to complete a particular grade and/or who drop out of school before completing even the primary cycle.

Repeating grades and dropping out exact a terrible personal toll on the pupils involved and absorb a large share of the limited resources available for education. Finding ways to minimize 'school wastage' must play a central role in any serious effort to reach the goal of Education for All (EFA).

Wastage is about missed opportunities for individuals, communities entire nations and regions of the world. It deprives developing countries of the ability to make the most efficient use of scarce resources and it takes its greatest toll on the most vulnerable groups in society. Finding ways to reduce school wastage must become an urgent priority for developing countries and their allies.

One of the great dangers facing the world today is the growing number of persons who are excluded from meaningful participation in the economic, social, political and cultural life of their communities. When critical masses of individuals or groups become marginalized, society itself becomes polarized. We appear to be moving toward a world in which wealth of all kinds—economic assets, social capital, political influence and knowledge—is being concentrated in the hands of a privileged few. Such a world is one that is neither efficient nor just nor safe.

The many roots of this polarization include factors ranging from the globalization of the economy to the dismantling of welfare states. Unfortunately, education, which is often seen as a means of promoting equality, can also contribute to inequality. In today's knowledge-based society, those who obtain a good basic education can continue to learn throughout their lives and thus remain economically viable, while those lacking a solid educational foundation are destined to fall further and further behind. Reducing school wastage is thus a critical necessity on ethical and economic grounds.

Low learning achievement, although not falling strictly into the traditional definition of internal efficiency, is considered these days as perhaps the most important, if not the ultimate, aspect of wastage in education.

This chapter addresses the problem of school wastage in developing countries, provides the latest data on trends in repetition and drop-out, and deals with three questions:

— How extensive is school wastage?

— What are its causes?

— What can be done to make schools more efficient?

The Goal of Education for All

The realization that basic education is both a necessity and a fundamental human right has long been recognized by the international community.

The Universal Declaration of Human Rights, adopted by the United Nations in 1948, asserted that 'everyone has a right to education', and subsequent international conferences and normative texts have reaffirmed this goal and sought to achieve it.

During International Literacy Year (1990), the World Conference on Education for All was convened in Jomtien, Thailand, to address concerns about inadequate provision of basic education, especially in the developing countries. The conference adopted the *World Declaration on Education for All* and agreed on a *Framework for Action to Meet Basic Learning Needs*. The Declaration begins by affirming that 'every person—child, youth and adult—shall be able to benefit from educational opportunities designed to meet their basic learning needs' and then outlines an 'expanded vision' of basic education that can make this possible.

The *Framework for Action* calls upon countries to adopt policies and practices that would ensure 'Universal access to, and completion, of primary education (or whatever higher level of education is considered as 'basic') by the year 2000'. It also urges countries to pursue 'Improvement in learning achievement such that an agreed percentage of an appropriate age cohort (*e.g.* 80 per cent of 14-year-olds) attains or surpasses a defined level of necessary learning achievement'.

Achieving the goals embraced at Jomtein requires not only that children be admitted to school when they are of age, but that they complete the entire primary cycle and, equally important, actually learn at an appropriate level. It is generally agreed that at least four years of schooling are necessary for pupils to acquire the basic literacy and numeracy skills needed to become continuing learners, so the following analysis gives particular attention to the proportion of pupils completing Grade 4 or reaching Grade 5.

Fig. 1: Global enrolment trends in primary education, 1970-95.

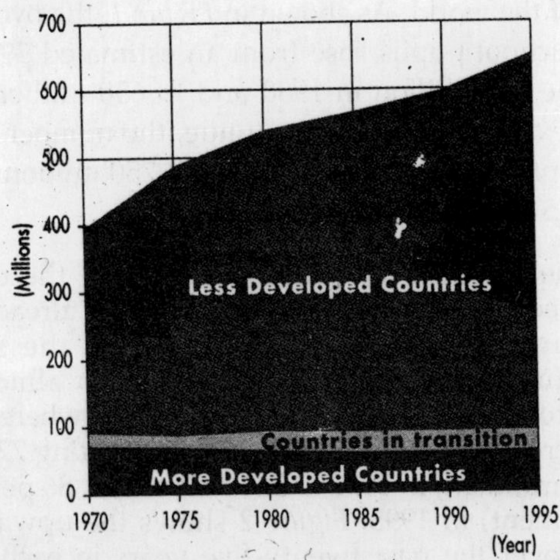

Source: UNESCO statistical database.

Fig. 2: Enrolment trends in primary education in the less developed regions, 1970-95.

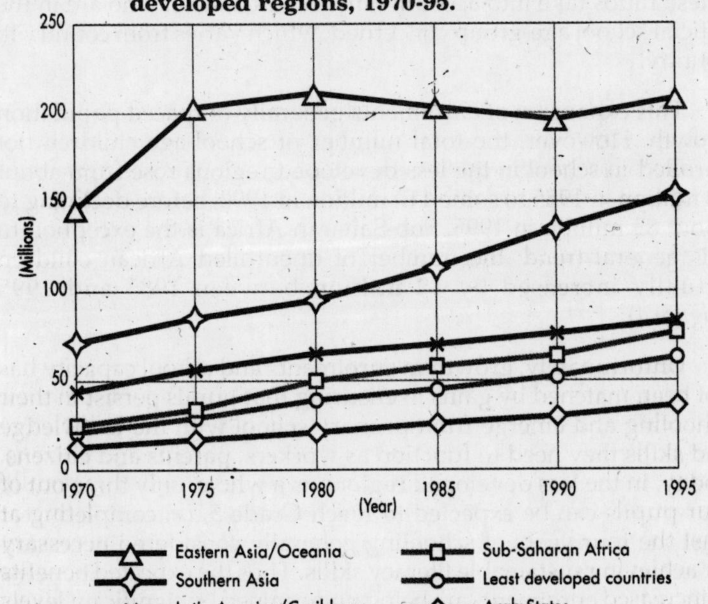

Source: UNESCO statistical database.

Considerable progress has been made over the last quarter century in expanding the capacity of primary school systems in all regions of the world. As shown in *Figure 1*, the overall number of primary school pupils rose from an estimated 396 million in 1970 to some 540 million in 1980 and to 650 million in 1995. If this rate of expansion were to continue, the number of pupils in the world's primary schools could reach 750 million by the year 2005 and 845 million by 2015.

Since the more developed countries and the countries in transition (see country lists in Annex II) had already achieved universal primary education before 1970, the subsequent expansion in primary school enrolments is almost entirely attributable to gains in the developing countries, where the number of pupils increased from 305 million (representing 77 per cent of the global enrolment) in 1970 to 561 million (*i.e.* 86 per cent of the global enrolment) in 1995. *Figure 2* shows the upward trend in enrolments over the past twenty-five years in each of the less developed regions. This general trend is also evident in the improved net enrolment ratios between 1985 and 1995 (*Figure 3*). These ratios take into account only those children who are in the official school age-group concerned, which varies from country to country.

This expansion of enrolments generally outpaced population growth. However, the total number of school-age children not enrolled in school in the less developed regions rose from about 90 million in 1985 to some 110 million in 1990, before declining to about 83 million in 1995. Sub-Saharan Africa is the exception to this general trend: the number of unenrolled African children actually increased by 12 million between 1985 and 1995 (*Figure 4*).

Unfortunately, growth in enrolments and school capacity has not been matched by gains in ensuring that pupils persist in their schooling and emerge from primary school with the knowledge and skills they need to function as workers, parents and citizens. Today, in the less developed regions as a whole, only three out of four pupils can be expected to reach Grade 5, *i.e.* completing at least the four years of schooling generally considered necessary for achieving sustainable literacy skills. Thus the expected benefits of increased enrolments are being undermined by significant levels of drop-out, an acute symptom of school wastage

Fig. 3: Estimated net enrolment ratios in primary education, by region and gender, 1985 and 1995.

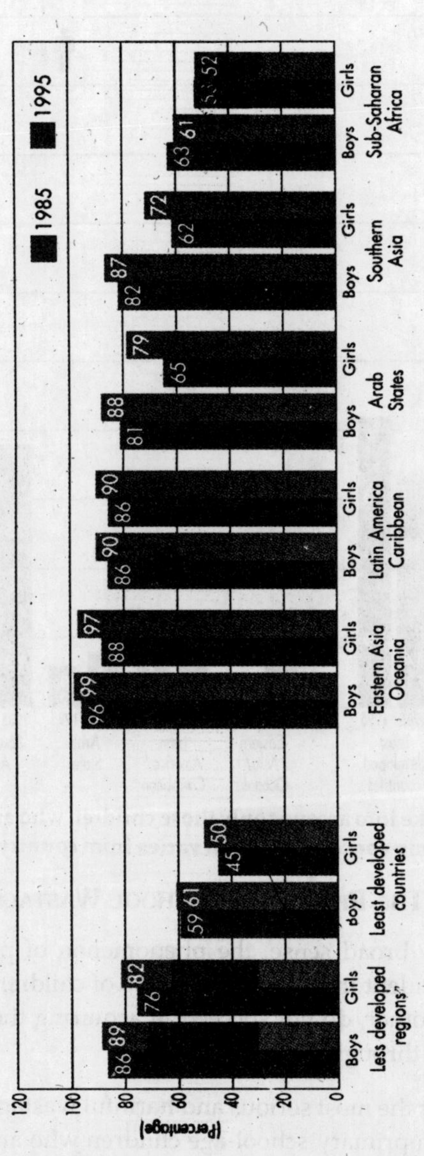

Fig. 4: Estimated unenrolled primary school-age population, by region and gender, 1985 and 1995.

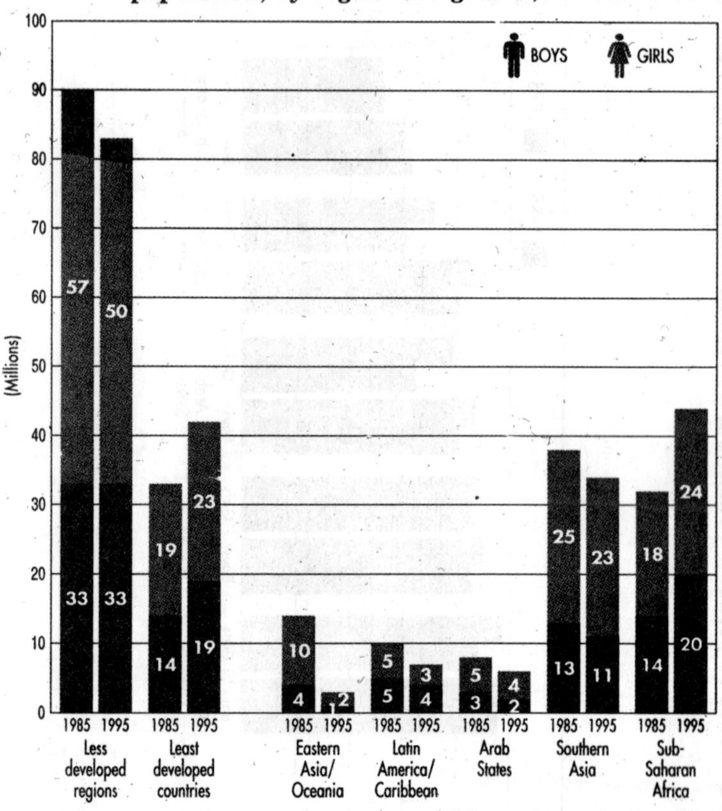

This figures take into account only those children who are in the official school age-group concerned, which varies from country to country.

THE PROBLEM OF SCHOOL WASTAGE

In a very broad sense, the phenomenon of primary-school wastage is evident in the large numbers of children who, for one reason on another, do not succeed in acquiring the full range of skills offered through primary schooling.

No doubt the most serious and harmful wastage is evident in the 84 million primary-school-age children who are not enrolled in school, of which three out of five are girls. (See Table—7.1).

Another, but less evident, form of wastage concerns the pupils who complete the primary cycle but fail to gain the intellectual, social, cultural and ethical knowledge and skills that schooling should provide. Surveys in industrialized and developing countries alike have found, for example, that a substantial, proportion of children complete their primary-school education without acquiring even an adequate mastery of reading. Children who never gain access to school and those who enrol but do not attain an adequate level of learning constitute a tragic waste of the human, social and economic potential of the countries concerned.

A more narrow, operational definition of school wastage refers to pupils who do not complete their schooling in the prescribed number of years either because they drop out of school entirely or because they repeat one or more grades. It is this concept of wastage—involving drop-outs and repeaters, especially at the primary school level—that is examined in this report.

Of course, wastage is also a serious problem in non-formal education programmes, such as adult literacy courses. However, data on such programmes are not readily available and the issues involved are often quite different from those affecting schooling. Consequently, this report focuses entirely on wastage in the formal primary-school system.

Measuring School Wastage

A major objective of Education for All is to ensure that children throughout the world have access to basic education, actually acquire basic literacy and numeracy skills, and develop the capacity for autonomous learning. Since the resources made available to schools for this important mission are often inadequate, they need to be efficient in moving pupils through each cycle of education in a timely fashion, See *Box 1:* How is school efficiency measured?

For the purpose of measuring the 'internal efficiency' of a school system, it is generally assumed that all pupils entering Grade 1 should complete the primary school cycle within a prescribed number of years. To the extent that pupils drop out of school or repeat grades, the system is considered inefficient. *Figure 5* shows the pronounced variation within and across the less developed regions of four 'synthetic indicators' that bring together

Table—7.1 Estimated Net Enrolment Ratios and Numbers of Primary-School-Age Population Out of School, Around 1995

	Coverage		*Net enrolment rates (%)*			*Unenrolled (in thousands) (coverage: all countries)*		
	No. of countries	*% school-age population*	*Total*	*Boys*	*Girls*	*Total*	*Boys*	*Girls*
World total	126	82	87.1	90.0	84.0	84,331	33,402	50,917
More developed regions	21	95	99.5	99.3	99.8	275	216	59
Countries in transition	15	64	96.6	96.8	96.6	947	471	476
Less developed regions	90	82	85.2	88.7	81.6	83,097	32,714	50,383
Sub-Saharan Africa	29	52	56.5	60.7	52.3	44,360	20,132	24,227
Arab States	16	74	83.6	88.3	78.7	6,743	2,437	4,305
Latin America/Caribbean	26	99	90.4	90.4	90.4	7,112	3,616	3,496
Eastern Asia/Oceania	13	85	98.0	98.7	97.3	3,608	1,206	2,401
Southern Asia	5	87	79.5	86.7	71.7	33,905	11,308	22,597
(Least developed countries)	29	78	55.6	60.8	50.4	41,607	18,585	23,022

Fig. 5: Internal efficiency of primary education in the less developed regions, around 1995.

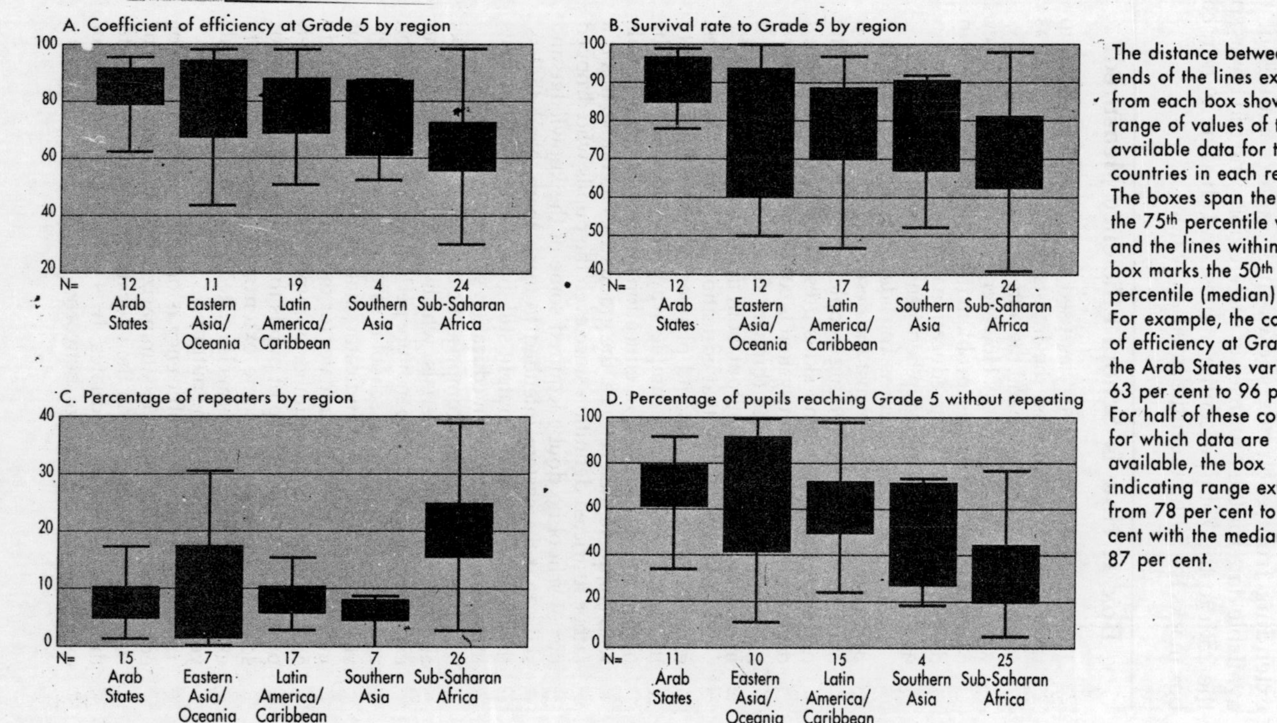

The distance between the ends of the lines extending from each box shows the range of values of the available data for the countries in each region. The boxes span the 25th to the 75th percentile values, and the lines within each box marks the 50th percentile (median) value. For example, the coefficient of efficiency at Grade 5 in the Arab States varies from 63 per cent to 96 per cent. For half of these countries for which data are available, the box indicating range extends from 78 per cent to 93 per cent with the median at 87 per cent.

data that reflect important aspects of the internal efficiency of primary school systems. The distance between the ends of the lines extending from each box shows the range of values of the available data for the countries in each region. The red boxes span the 25th to the 75th percentile values, and the line within each box marks the 50th percentile (median) value.

Box 1. How is School Efficiency Measured?

The concept of 'efficiency', as used by economists, refers to the relationship between the inputs into a system (such as seeds, lumber or pupils) and the outputs from that system (e.g. wheat, chairs or graduates). However, measuring the efficiency of education systems is problematic due to difficulties in defining and measuring educational outputs, as well as in quantifying the relationship between inputs and outputs.

An education system is considered to be sufficient if it produces at a minimum cost the desired output in terms of a maximum number of young people who have acquired the necessary knowledge and skills prescribed by society. Stated differently, an education system is considered efficient if for a given input of resources (human, financial and material) it maximizes the desired output, both in quantity and quality.

While recognizing that education has various objectives, educational statisticians and planners measure the output of the school system in a simple way. They assume that the output of a given cycle of education is the number of pupils who complete the cycle, i.e. the graduates. Of course, this is a rather restricted definition since even the pupils who dropped out of school no doubt acquired some of the knowledge and skills that the system intended to teach them. Nevertheless, this way of measuring output still gives some useful insights into the functioning of an education system.

Educational inputs comprise the buildings, teachers, books and other learning materials, which may be aggregated and expressed in terms of expenditure per pupil per year. One pupil who spends one year at school is said to have spent on pupil-year. The usual input indicator that corresponds to output measured in terms of graduates (or those who complete Grade 5, for example) is the number of pupil-years used by a given pupil cohort (i.e. a group of pupils that enters the first year of school together). To some extent, the amount of inputs expressed in monetary terms is related to the number of pupil-years used to produce the output.

The Coefficient of efficiency is one synthetic indicator of educational efficiency. It summarizes the consequences of repetition and drop-out in the educational process leading to the 'production' of graduates. It is calculated as the ratio, expressed as a percentage, between:

(i) the optimal number of pupil-years that would be required to complete a cycle of education if no pupils repeated grades or dropped out; and

(ii) the actual number of pupil-years spent by a pupil cohort to complete the cycle. Any additional years spent to graduate pupils beyond the prescribed duration of a cycle of studies constitute an inefficient allocation of resources, yielding a coefficient of efficiency of less than 100 per cent (or unity).

Thus if it takes a cohort on average six years to complete a four-year primary cycle, the coefficient of efficiency would be 0.66, indicating a system operating at only two-thirds efficiency and 'wasting' one-third of its resources on repeaters and drop-outs.

The input-output ratio, which is the reciprocal of coefficient of efficiency, is often used as an alternative measure. The optimum input-output point is also unity, but any value greater than one indicates inefficiency. In the example above, the input-output ratio would be 1.5 (6 divided by 4).
Since the length of the primary school cycle varies from country to country, it may not be meaningful to make comparisons of school efficiency across countries. To improve comparability, therefore, the analysis of school wastage in this report is based on internal efficiency indicators that have been calculated using Grade 5 as the common reference point, as this is the grade at which a pupil is assumed to have achieved sustainable literacy.

The converse of 'drop-out' is 'survival' or 'retention', meaning that the pupil survives, or is retained, in the primary cycle. The survival rate used in this report indicates the percentage of pupils who enrol together in Grade 1 (a pupil cohort) that eventually reaches Grade 5.

Fig. 6: Apparent survival rates to Grade 5 by region, 1994-95

	Grade 1	*Grade 2*	*Grade 3*	*Grade 4*	*Grade 5*
More developed regions (N = 17) 82 %	100 %	100 %	99 %	99 %	99 %
Less developed regions (N = 78) 89 %	100 %	88 %	84 %	79 %	75 %
Least developed countries (N = 25) 42 %	100 %	76 %	70 %	62 %	56 %

figure Contd...

	1	2	3	4	5
Arab States (N = 14) 69 %	100 %	99 %	97 %	96 %	93 %
Eastern Asia/ Oceania (N = 12) 90 %	100 %	95 %	92 %	89 %	86 %
Southern Asia (N = 5) 78 %	100 %	82 %	76 %	69 %	65 %
Latin America/ Caribbean (N = 17) 90 %	100 %	83 %	77 %	71 %	67 %
Sub-Saharan Africa (N = 27) 81 %	100 %	82 %	78 %	72 %	67 %

In the first column, N is the number of countries in the region for which pertinent data are available for calculating the movement of a pupil cohort through five years of schooling. The percentage next to it shows the share of these countries in the total enrolment of the region.

Box 2. Analysing School Wastage

To measure internal efficiency and wastage in education, statisticians and planners use techniques similar to those of cohort analysis in demography. A 'cohort' is a group of persons who jointly experience a series of specific events over a period of time. Accordingly, a pupil cohort is a group of pupils who enter the first grade of a school cycle in the same year and who normally move through the cycle together. However, the pupils experience promotion, repetition, drop-out or successful completion of the final grade each in his or her own way.

There are three ways to analyse wastage in education by examining data on the flow of pupils in a cohort, depending on what data are available. The best way to obtain an accurate assessment of wastage is through the true cohort method, which involves either a longitudinal study of a pupil cohort through a full educational cycle or a retrospective study of school records to retrace the flow of pupils through the grades over the years. This method, however, is costly and time-consuming, and requires, reliable school records with data on individual pupils. Consequently, this method is not generally used.

In the absence of individual pupil data, the apparent cohort method can be used when there are no data on repetition. School wastage is assessed using enrolment data by grade for at least two consecutive years. Enrolment in Grade 1 in a given year is compared with enrolment in the consecutive grades during the following years and any decrease in enrolment from one grade to the next is assumed to be due to drop-out. This commonly used method produces very approximative estimates of efficiency and wastage. Its main weakness is that it ignores repetition, so this method is appropriate only for countries that practice automatic promotion.

The reconstructed cohort method is less dependent on detailed data over time. Enrolment data by grade for two consecutive years and data on repetition by grade from the first to the second year are sufficient to measure the three main flow-rates: promotion, repetition and drop-out. These rates can be analysed by grade to study the patterns of repetition and drop-out. They can also be used to reconstruct the pupil cohort flow to derive other indicators of internal efficiency. (See also Box 1).

Dropping out of School

An obvious an blatant form of wastage involves pupils who start school but drop out before they reach a level of sustainable literacy and numeracy.

Drop-out at the primary level is virtually non-existent in industrialized countries because they enforce compulsory education laws. In the less developed regions, however, early drop-out is a major problem. Of the approximately 96 million pupils who entered school for the first time in 1995, one quarter (24 million) are likely to abandon their schooling before they reach Grade 5.

Figure 6 shows the apparent survival rates to Grade 5 of pupils in different regions of the world based on data for 1994-95 reported by a substantial number of countries. The more developed regions show survival rates that approach 100 per cent, but in the less developed regions as a whole, only three out of four pupils reach Grade 5. The situation in the cross-regional sub-group of least developed countries is even more grim, with barely half (56 per cent) of the pupils remaining in school after Grade 4.

A closer analysis of the survival rates, shows that boys persist in school at slightly higher rates than do girls, except in Latin America and the Caribbean, and in the more developed regions (*Figure 7*). However, the more important disparity between boys and girls is evident in the overall enrolment figures for the less developed regions. Three-quarters of the 8 million school entrance-age children who did not enter school in 1994-95 were girls (*Figure 8*). This gender disparity at the beginning of schooling generally continues throughout the primary cycle, as can be seen in the gap between the net enrolment ratios of boys and girls (*Figure 9*).

Fig. 7: Apparent survival rates to Grade 5, by region and gender, 1994-95.

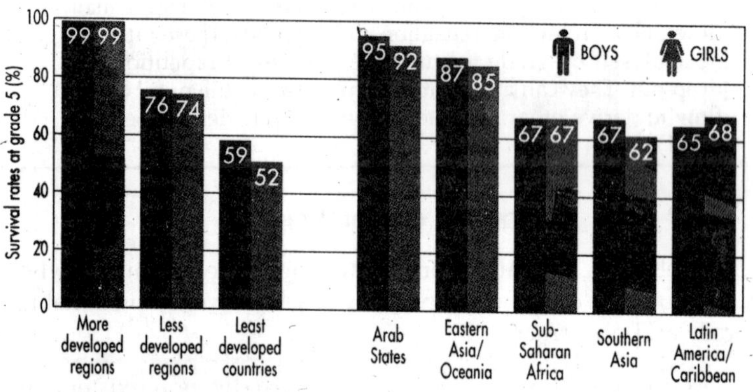

As seen earlier (*Figure 6*), much dropping out of school occurs between the first and second grades. In the less developed regions taken together, nearly half of all drop-out occurs before pupils reach Grade 2. The exception is the Arab States, where the overall survival rate to Grade 5 is high, but most drop-out occurs between Grades 4 and 5.

The pattern of substantial drop-out occurring at the beginning of the primary school cycle is particularly distressing because pupils with only a year or two of schooling leave in a state of near literacy.

Fig. 8: Population of primary-school entrance age in the less developed regions around 1995; access, expected survival and drop-out by gender.

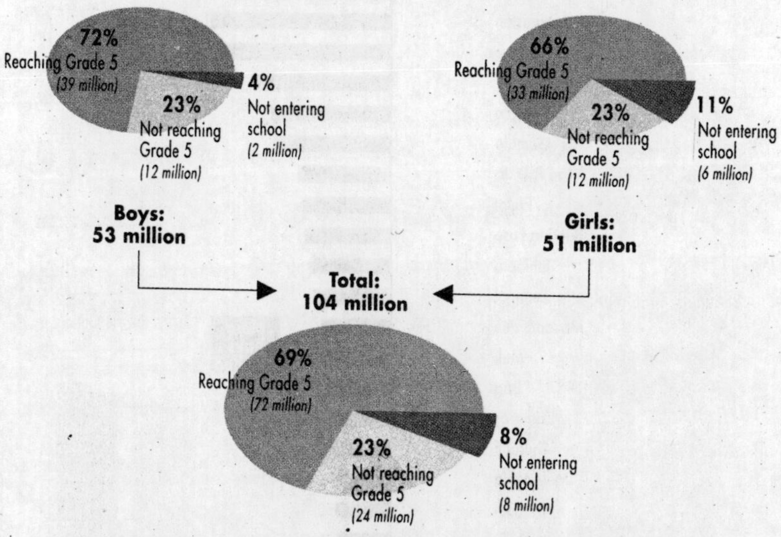

However, the overall survival rates to Grade 5 appear to be improving in a number of countries for which data are available.

Box 3. What Happens to Drop-Outs?

Rural schools often have higher drop-out rates than do urban schools. An interesting tracer study in China looked into what happened to rural and urban children who dropped out of school. Among the primary school drop-outs in rural areas, nearly half (47.5 per cent) worked on farms, while 7.5 per cent were in part-time or other employment, compared with 27.3 per cent of the urban drop-outs who were in part-time employment. In both cases over one-third were staying at home.

Among children who dropped out of rural junior secondary schools, three out of five (61.2 per cent) were doing farm work, one out of five (21.5 per cent) had full-time or part-time jobs and just over 11 per cent were jobless. In urban areas the jobless rate doubled to slightly more than 22 per cent; 57 per cent had full-time or part-time jobs.

These findings, which were part of the Asian Regional Study of Wastage in Education, reflect the way socio-economic and environmental factors affect dropping out. This was further illustrated through a sample survey conducted in sixty of China's

Fig. 9: Gap between net enrolment ratios of boys and girls, 1995.

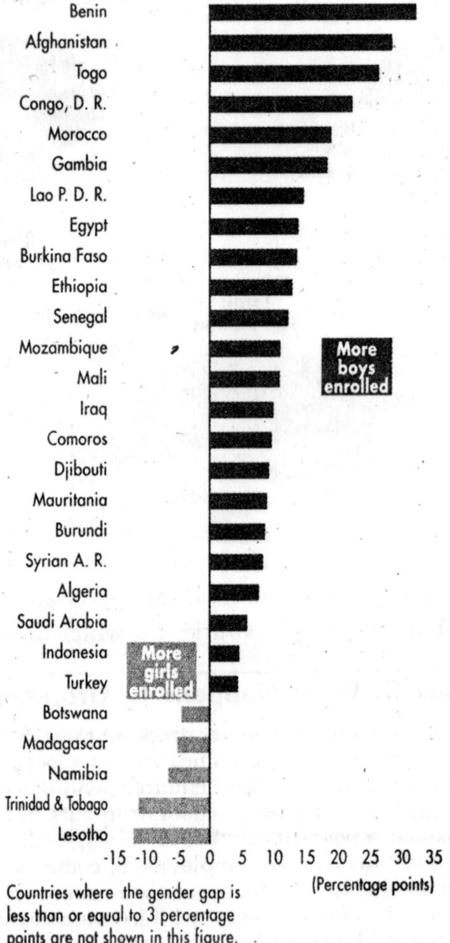

Countries where the gender gap is less than or equal to 3 percentage points are not shown in this figure.

counties. It showed that the drop-out rate in counties with a low average per capita income (less than 300 yuan) was 4.3 per cent, while counties with an average per capita income of 300 to 800 yuan had a drop-out rate of 1.1 per cent. In counties with average per capita income of more than 800 yuan, the drop-out rate was 0.3 per cent.

Box 4. Does Repeating Grades Help Pupils?

Public schools in the United States have a long tradition of having pupils repeat grades when they are not succeeding in their schoolwork. However, dozens of studies over the last two decades have shown that retaining pupils in a grade can be counter-productive, Lorrie Shepard and Mary Lee Smith concluded in a review of research on the subject. Contrary to popular beliefs, repeating a grade does not help students gain ground academically and has a negative impact on social adjustment and self-esteem.

No matter how much parents and educators try to portray repetition in a constructive light, pupils who do not progress to the next grade level with their peers invariably struggle with problems of self-esteem. Not surprisingly, researchers have found that repeaters tend to develop highly negative attitudes toward school. Repeating early grades frequently leads to further retention down the road, which in turn can lead to dropping out entirely. A report by the Carnegie Council on Adolescent Development estimated that a single grade retention increases the likelihood of drop-out by 40 to 50 per cent. A second one raises the risk to 90 per cent.

During the 1980s, the public school system in New York City instituted a 'promotional gates' programme that required pupils in Grades 4 and 8 to attain specified minimum scores on standardized reading and mathematics tests before moving on to the next grade. The programme was scrapped a few years later because the retained students who received no special academic support the following year continued to have academic difficulties. The presence of substantial numbers of older students repeating classes turned out to be disruptive and the repeaters dropped out in significant numbers.

In an article in the journal Phi Delta Kappan (November 1997), Linda Darling-Hammond and Beverly Falk suggest three reasons why repetition does not work:

- Just because a pupil repeats an academic year does not mean that his or her natural social and intellectual cycles will be halted. Development is continuous, uneven and multi-dimensional, they write, and young children are often better served by a school structure that supports their continues progress.
- The norm-referenced standardized tests used to make retention decisions are designed to produce a ranking of pupils, not to determine whether students have mastered a specific body of knowledge. The tests can easily underestimate a pupil's knowledge, especially when pupils are confused by the artificial format of such tests.

- Grade repetition presumes that the problem, if there is one, is attributable to the child rather than factors such as the quality of teaching or the school setting. Significantly, retention rates for children from low-income families are at least twice as high as those for children from high-income families. Since children from poor families are less likely to receive instruction from well-qualified and highly effective teachers, their academic difficulties are exacerbated, not solved, by grade retention.

Repeating Grades

Another form of school wastage occurs when pupils have to repeat grades. In developing countries especially, this is often a prelude to drop-out.

School systems around the world differ widely in their policies toward pupils who fail to master the work appropriate to a particular grade level. In a majority of countries, both developed and developing, educators require such pupils to repeat the grade in order to give them additional time to learn material that they failed to master the first time around. Repetition is thus seen as a remedy for slow learners. The practice is typically applied in Grade 1 out of a conviction that it is important for pupils to get off to a good start in their education. However, repeating the final primary grade is also widespread in countries where admission to secondary school is based on passing an end-of-primary-school examination.

A minority of countries appear to believe that repetition creates more problems than it solves and therefore follow a policy of automatic promotion. Accordingly, pupils proceed to the next grade even when they have not mastered the material of the previous grade. Some educators argue that pupils who did not learn something the first time are not likely to benefit from repeating the same academic year. A wiser policy, they argue, is to provide such pupils additional assistance and allow them to proceed to the next grade with their peers.

The data in Table—7.2 show that in the less developed regions together, about eight per cent of all pupils enrolled in primary school around 1995 were repeaters, and nearly one out of three pupils in Grade 1 was a repeater. Overall repetition rates are highest in sub-Saharan Africa and in Latin American and the Caribbean.

Table—7.2 Estimated Number of Repeaters in Primary Education, by Region, Around 1985 and 1995

Region	Estimated number of repeaters around 1985		Estimated number of repeaters around 1995			
	All grades		All grades		First grade only	
	(in thousand	*As % of enrolment*	*(in thousand*	*As % of enrolment*	*(in thousand*	*As % ofAll repeaters*
Less developed regions	50,521	10	42,902	8	13,012	30
Sub-Saharan Africa	9,616	17	11,640	16	3,551	31
Arab States	2,550	10	2,814	8	485	17
Latin America/Caribbean	10,123	14	10,221	13	3,112	30
Eastern Asia/Oceania	15,142	7	6,936	3	3,077	44
Southern Asia	13,091	12	11,291	7	2,786	25
(Least developed countries)	7,505	16	11,220	18	3,964	35

Because the incidence of repetition is largely determined by the attitudes and practices of educators in each country, the magnitude of repetition can vary considerably even among countries of comparable levels of educational and economic development. For example, Niger and Madagascar are both in the sub-group of least developed countries: each has a large proportion of people living on less than US$1 a day and a primary net enrolment ratio of less than 50 per cent. Nevertheless, Niger has a repetition rate of only 16 per cent, compared with 32 per cent in Madagascar.

Repetition rates appear to be declining in many developing countries. *Figure 10* shows that the percentage of pupils repeating their present grade declined between 1985 and 1995 in all less developed regions. However, this general trend did not apply to the sub-set of least developed countries, where the percentage of repeaters increased.

Repetition, like drop-out, tends to be more prevalent in the first and in the final grades of the primary school cycle, but repetition patterns vary considerably both within and between different countries (*Figure 11*) and across the several regions (*Figure 12*). In general, however, the percentage of repeaters in Grade 1 exceeds the percentage of repeaters in all grades together (*Figure 13*).

The proportion of pupils reaching Grade 5 without repeating a grade also varies widely among countries. *Figure 14* shows the gap between total survival rates to Grade 5 (*i.e.* including repeaters) and survival rates to Grade 5 without repetition for selected countries around 1994-95. The gap ranges from as little as two percentage points in Kiribati to as much as 51 percentage points in Lesotho. In Chad, less than one in ten pupils reach Grade 5 without repeating a grade, while four in ten pupils finally reach Grade 5 after repeating at least one grade.

Box 5. Child Labour and Wastage

In many developing countries, child labour is a major obstacle both to providing universal access to schooling and to reducing school wastage.

The International Labour Organisation (ILO) estimates that 250 million children between the ages of 5 and 14 are toiling in the workforce of developing countries. About half of these children work full-time, while the rest combine work with schooling or other non-economic activities. However, these estimates do not take into account children who work full-time for their families doing agricultural work or taking care of younger siblings. ILO statistics show that more boys work than girls by a margin of three to two, but the data probably underestimate the unpaid domestic work of girls.

In absolute numbers, Asia accounts for three out of five child workers, whereas Africa accounts for one out of three. Some 7 per cent live in Latin America and less than 1 per cent in Oceania. In relative terms, however, child labour is most common in Africa, where an estimated 41 per cent of children aged 5 to 14 are working, compared with about 21 per cent in Asia, 17 per cent in Latin America and 10 per cent in Oceania. In all regions, the proportion of child workers is much higher in rural areas than in urban centres.

Child labour and absenteeism from school feed on each other. Thus measures to reduce child labour or to improve the coverage and quality of schooling tend to produce benefits in both areas. Many countries are making serious efforts to reduce child labour. The International Programme on the Elimination of Child Labour (IPEC), established by ILO, offers assistance to countries with explicit national programmes to combat the problem. ILO and the United Nations Children's Fund (UNICEF) recently committed themselves to working together to eliminate child labour and ILO is preparing a draft convention that will strengthen the international legal framework against the problem.

Poverty is generally seen as the most compelling reason for children to work, but researchers have found that poverty need not cause child labour. There are many examples of regions of poor countries that have abolished the practice, such as Kerala State in India.

Research has also shown that the 'economic irreplaceability' argument for-using child workers also collapses under close scrutiny. ILO has found, for example, that the expected savings on the cost of labour by using children to produce bangles and carpets are surprisingly small, less than 5 and 10 per cent, respectively, of the market price. Such cost savings could easily be compensated for by a small levy on the consumer price.

Laws governing compulsory schooling and the minimum age for employment are interdependent, so enforcing one contributes to enforcement of the other. There are also important long-term benefits from such a two-pronged approach. Educated individuals are more likely to be productive and successful workers, to have higher educational aspirations for their children and to understand that child labour is actually a weight on society.

Fig. 10: Percentage of repeaters in primary education, by region, 1985 and 1995.

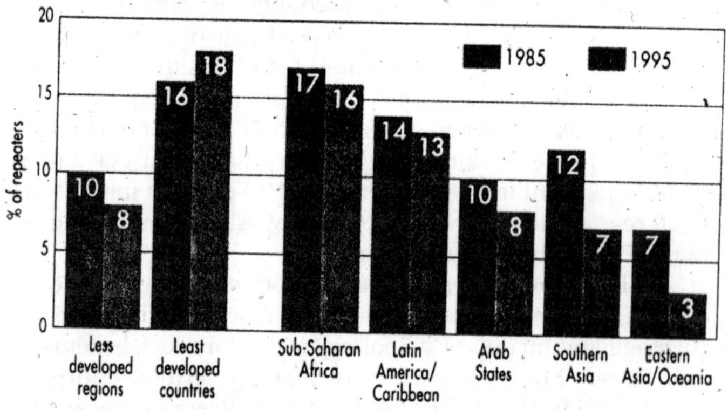

Combined Effects of Drop-out and Repetition

Under optimal circumstances, every primary-school pupil would spend one year at each grade level and compete a five-year cycle in five years, or a six-year cycle in six years, and so on. When pupils repeat grades or drop out, however, the average number of 'pupil-year' required to move pupils through the cycle exceeds the prescribed number of years. *Figure 15* shows the average number of pupil-years required for completion of Grade 5 in selected countries around 1995. The numbers range from a low of 5 years in Jordan to a high of 14 years in Chad.

In many countries the proportion of wastage due to drop-out as compared to repetition differs for boys and girls (*Figure 16*). For example, drop-out is a more significant factor for girls than for boys in countries such as Indonesia, Senegal, Guinea and Togo, whereas it is more important factor for boys than for girls in Colombia and Lesotho.

The High Cost of Wastage

Persistent high rates of wastage impose enormous costs on education systems—and also on the individuals and societies that they serve.

Fig. 11: Pattern of repetition be grade in primary school, selected countries, latest year available.

Pattern 1. **Repetition rates increase in the final grade.**

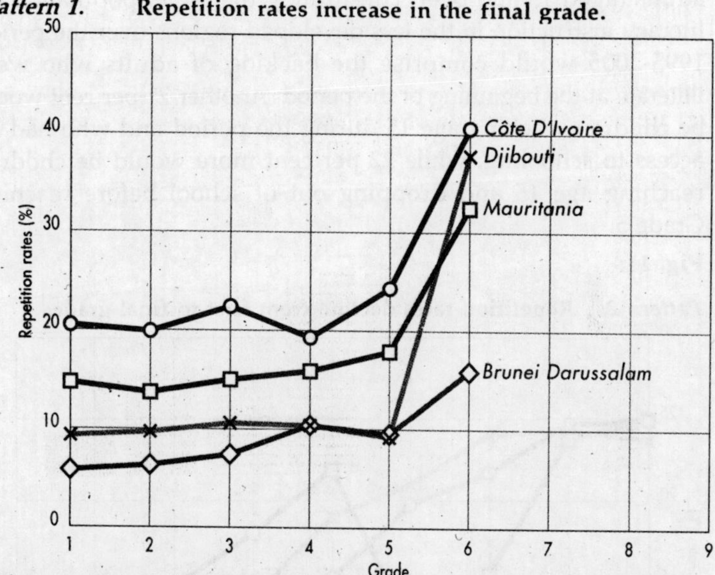

Other countries with the same patterns:

Benin, Burkina Faso, Comoros, Guinea, Malawi, Mali, Senegal, Egypt, Tunisia, Solomon Islands.

Educational Costs

Wastage substantially reduces the capacity of school systems to meet the objectives of education for all. Pupils who require more than one year to complete a grade take up space, teaching time, textbooks and other resources that could be devoted instead to other pupils. In Cambodia, for example, where four out of every ten pupils at any given time are repeaters, the Asian Development Bank estimated that serving these repeaters requires 10,000 additional teachers and 5,000 more classrooms, *i.e.* 20 per cent of the existing stock. Furthermore when many pupils repeat grades, some classes become abnormally large, making the teaching and learning conditions difficult for everyone.

Wastage has important long-term effects on patterns of adult illiteracy. It is widely recognized that children who drop out of school before acquiring basic literacy and numeracy skills frequently relapse into illiteracy. Estimates based on a simulation model (see *Figure 17*) project that 57 per cent of the illiterate adults (aged 15 and over) constituting the target population for literacy instruction in the less developed regions over the period 1995-2005 would comprise the backlog of adults who were illiterate at the beginning of the period. Another 21 per cent would be children reaching age 15 during the period and who had no access to schooling, while 22 per cent more would be children reaching age 15 and dropping out of school before reaching Grade 5.

Fig. 11:

Pattern 2. **Repetition rates decline from first to final grades.**

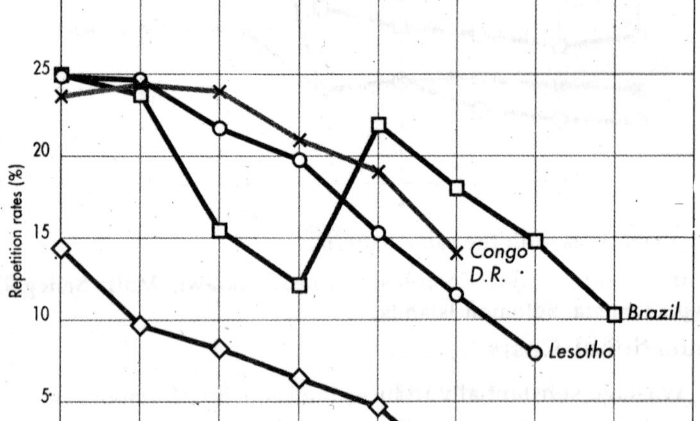

Other countries with the same patterns:

Congo, Eritrea, Ethiopia, Lesotho, Madagascar, Mozambique, Namibia, Swaziland, Togo, Bahrain, Morocco, Saudi Arabia, Syrian A.R, China, Lao P.D.R., Kiribati, Argentina, Colmbia, Costa Rica, Ecuador, El Salvador, Honduras, Mexico, Nicaragua, Paraguay, Peru, Uruguay.

One of the presumed benefits of repetition is to ensure that pupils in each grade have attained more or less the same level of learning an can learn at about the same pace. This assumption is frequently undermined, however, when teachers end up dealing with pupils of varying ages. A recent report on the age of pupils by grade in Latin America shows that Grade 1 teachers had pupils ranging in age from 5 to 8, while a similar study in Kenya revealed an age range in Grade 1 from 2 to 16. In some countries, the age range found in the early grades is due both to repetition and to the practice of admitting children who are younger and older than the official entry age. (*Figure 18*).

Fig. 11:

Pattern 3. **Repetition rates remain about the same in all grades.**

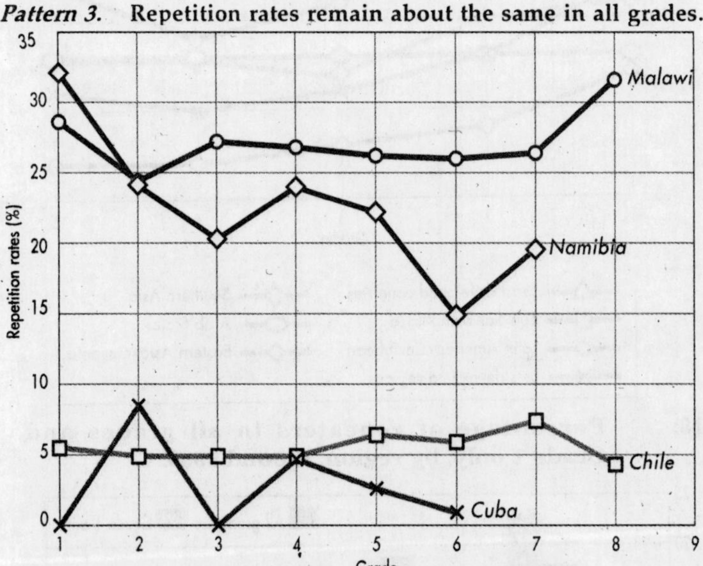

Other countries and territories with the same patterns:

Chad, Ethiopia, Algeria, Jordon, Oman, Palestine, Qatar, United Arab Emirates, Bhutan, Iran, I.R., Sri Lanka, Belize, Guyana.

Many teachers and school administrators consider it normal for substantial proportions of pupils to be held back. They take pride in high repetition rates and see them as evidence of their commitment to high standards. One educators, however, see them as an indictment of the teaching that the retained pupils received. In any case, what some see as a yardstick of academic quality can have pedagogical, social and personal consequences that are quite destructive.

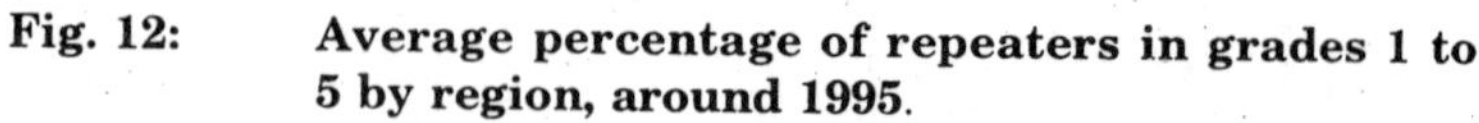

Fig. 12: Average percentage of repeaters in grades 1 to 5 by region, around 1995.

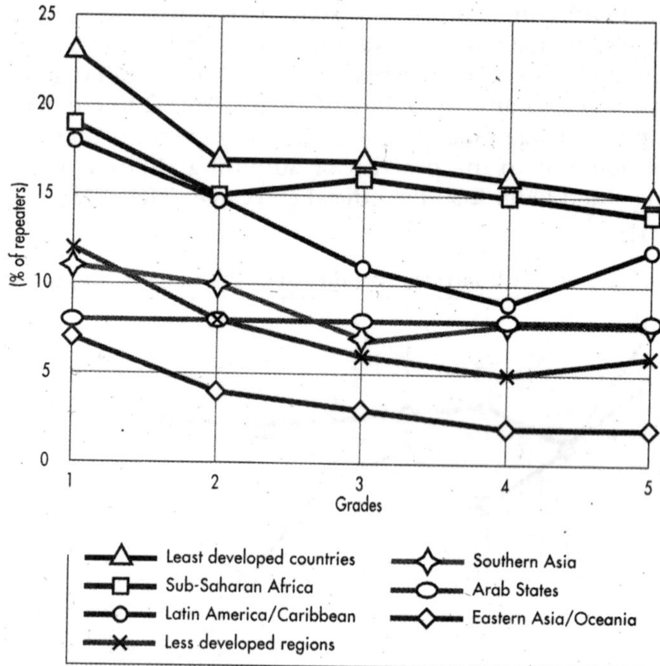

Fig. 13: Percentage of repeaters in all grades and Grade 1 only, by region, around 1995.

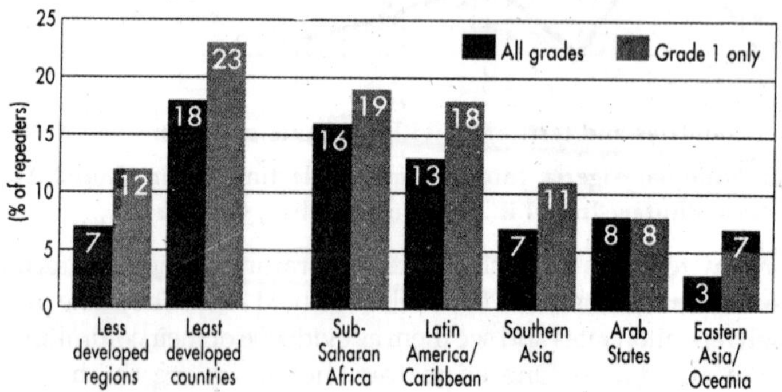

Fig. 14: Percentage of cohort surviving to Grade 5 in selected countries: total and without grade repetition, 1994-95.

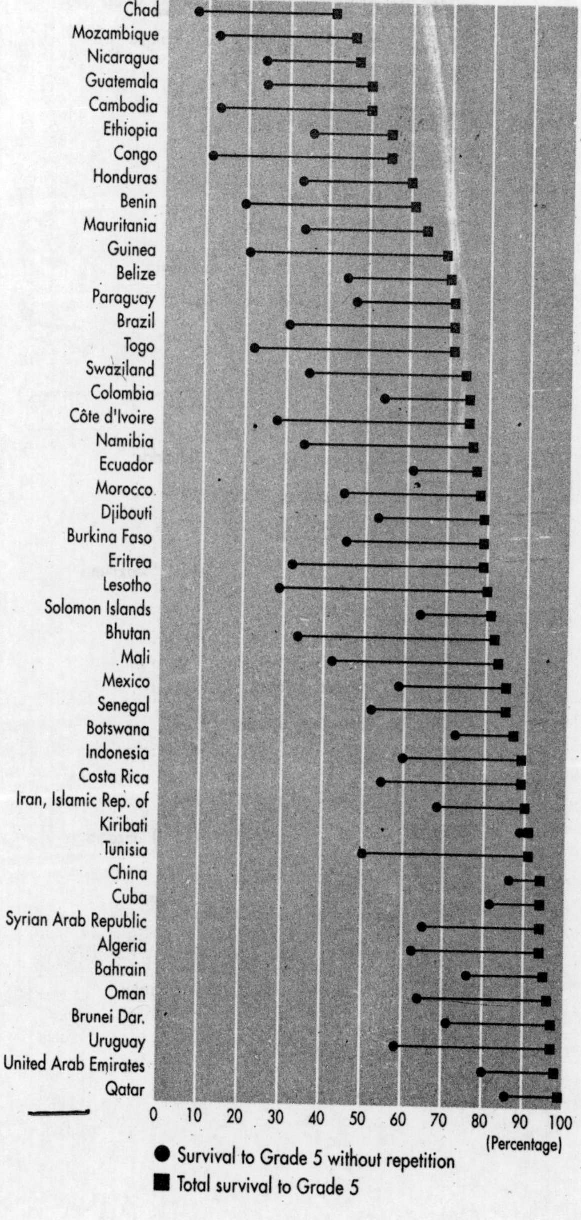

Fig. 15: Average number of years pupils take to complete Grade 5 in selected countries, around 1995.

Fig. 16: Varying proportion of total wastage occurring before Grade 5 due to drop-out and repetition, by gender, in selected countries, around 1995.

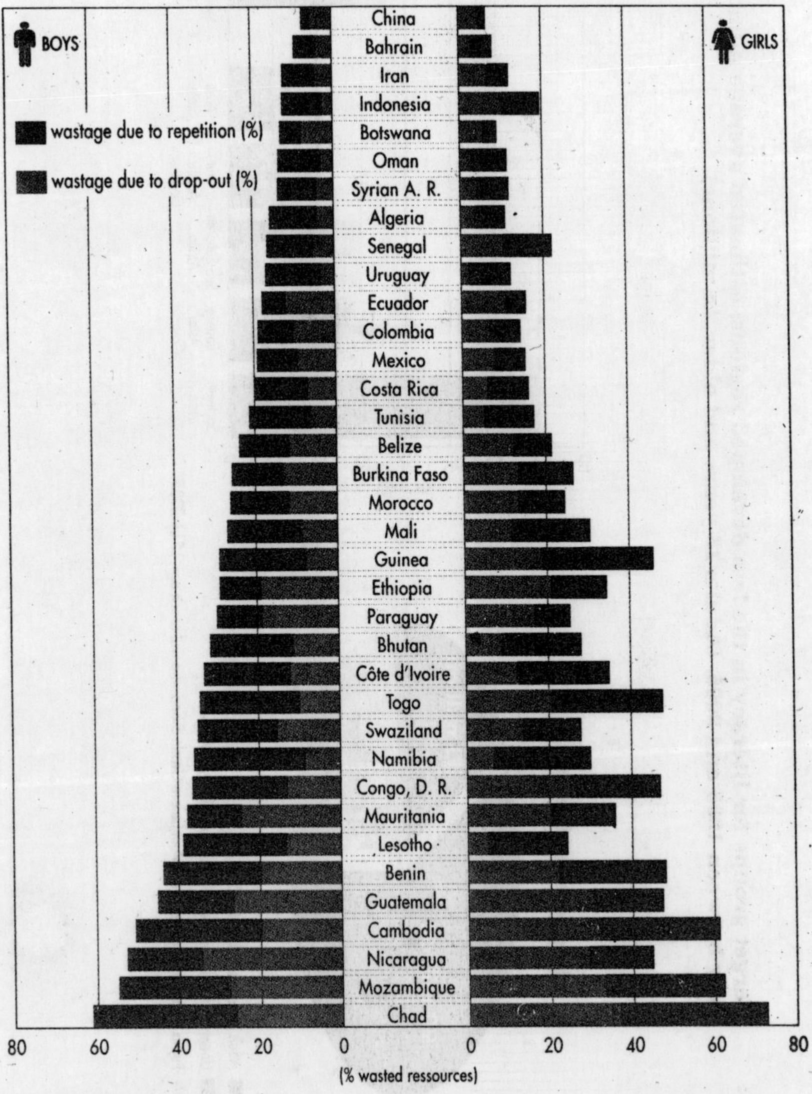

Fig. 17: Target groups for literacy in the less developed regions: estimated average number per year between 1995 and 2005. (Adults 15 years and older, in millions).

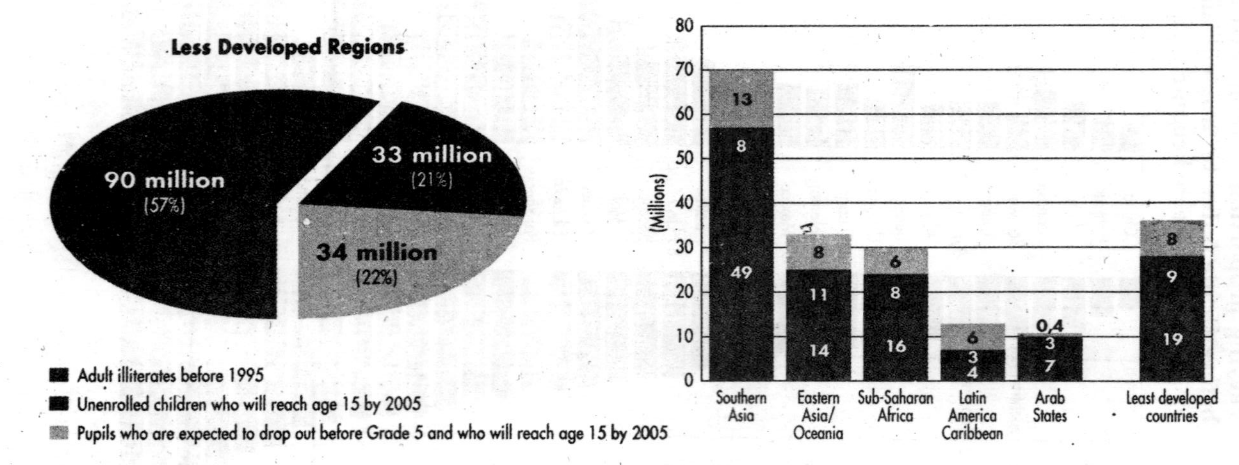

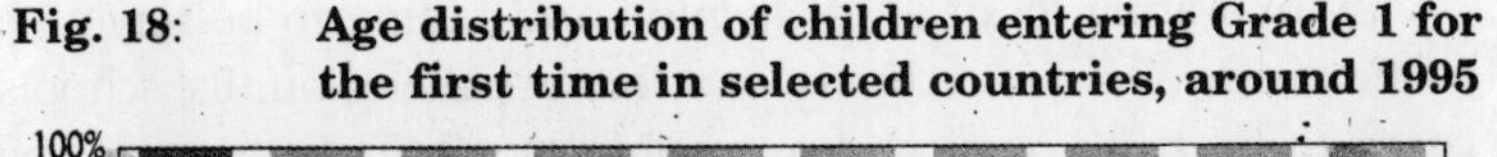

Fig. 18: Age distribution of children entering Grade 1 for the first time in selected countries, around 1995

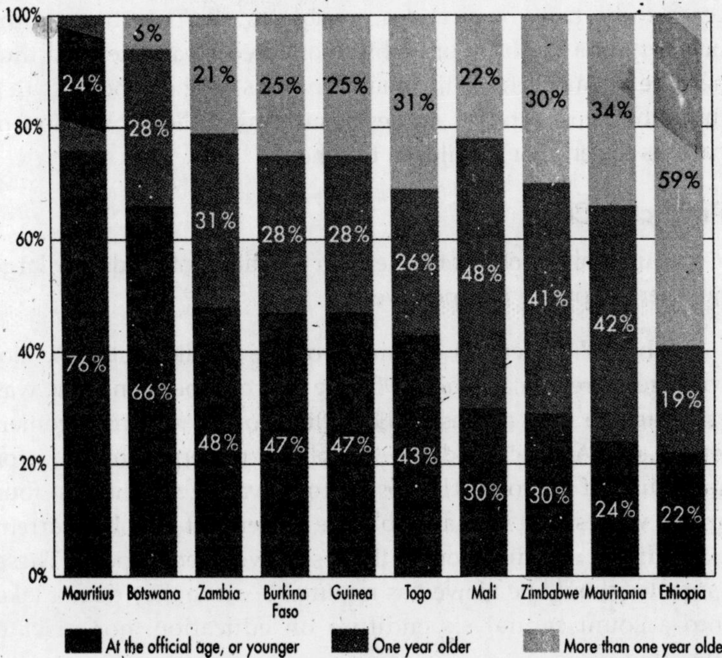

Source: National education statistical information systems (NESIS), Paris UNESCO/DAE, 1996.

Anecdotal evidence suggests that decisions to hold pupils back are sometimes made on capricious and arbitrary grounds that have little to do with actual pupil performance. Teachers often favour pupils who readily follow rules and give more attention to the brightest pupils at the expense of the others, including pupils who are competent but not outstanding. A study carried out in rural primary schools in Honduras, for example, found that 20 per cent of pupils with sufficient qualifications had not been promoted, while another study in rural Brazil found no significant relation between actual performance and promotion. School systems in many countries lack clear definitions and established procedures for assessing pupil performance and making promotion decisions.

By operating in an elitist fashion and failing to be sensitive to the needs of many ordinary and low-achieving pupils, schools cease to be truly open and accessible to all. They become the property of a minority of highly motivated local elites and thus become alienated from the community as a whole. Schools that limit the prospects for success undermine the motivation of parents to send their children to school.

Financial Costs

Maintaining policies that lead to repetition of grades by large numbers of pupils is expensive.

Table—7.3 presents estimates of the public cost of school wastage by region around 1995. The cost of repetition alone was estimated to total at least US$6 billion for all regions together, with Latin America and the Caribbean region accounting for about half of the total. The cost of total wastage in the first four grades was estimated to absorb some 16 per cent of public current expenditure on education in the less developed regions. These estimates should be viewed as minimal because they do not take into account capital expenditure on education, nor private spending.

Regardless of its pedagogical effects, repeating grades is inefficient because, it increases the per pupil cost of schooling without increasing the number of graduates produced. Resources devoted to a repeater are resources that could have been used either to permit another child to enter school or to improve the quality of instruction for pupils already there. From the data presented in *Figure 16*, for instance it appears that Mozambique's school system is operating at less than half efficiency and Chad's system at about one-third efficiency.

Economic Social and Personal Costs

One of the premises of investment in education is that it makes an important and measurable contribution to the economic growth of society, in particular by improving the productivity of labour. A close parallel exists between the rate of economic growth of a country and the overall level of education of its active

Table—7.3 Estimated Public Cost of Educational Wastage by Region Around 1995

Region	Estimated cost of repetition			Education public current expenditure		
	Total Cases of Repetition (in thousands	Cost per Pupil US$	Total cost (million US$)	Total (million US$)	Spent on Wastage before Grade 5 (million US$)	(% of total)
Less developed regions	42,902	...	...	...	...	15.8
Sub-Saharan Africa	11,640	49	570	18,800	6,167	32.8
Arab States	2,814	...	...	27,500	3,460	12.6
Latin America/Caribbean	10,221	312	3,189	72,800	19,393	26.6
Eastern Asia/Oceania	6,936	89	617	59,900	6,139	10.2
Southern Asia	11,291	121	1,366	18,800	...	...
(Least developed countries)	11,220	19	213	5,300	2,005	37.8

population. This correlation has been documented both in advanced industrial societies and in developing countries where the agricultural sector remains dominant. Whereas reliance on agriculture has frequently been a force for keeping children out of school, modern agricultural practices require more skilled, albeit fewer, workers.

In view of the importance of the agricultural sector for the economy of most poor countries, it is clear that the persistence of substantial school wastage is contrary to the economic interest of these countries, especially since wastage tends to be more pronounced in rural than in urban areas. Although the level of education is not the only factor involved in agricultural production, the failure to enable many rural young people to master basic skills undermines other initiatives to stimulate rural development.

Children who drop out of school before acquiring sustainable reading and writing skills frequently relapse into illiteracy. Thus dropping out undermines efforts to reduce adult illiteracy—like trying to drain a sink that is being filled at the same time by the tap. Children and adolescents out of school in urban areas are also more vulnerable to the attractions of street life and organised gangs of children, which contributes to problems of delinquency and crime. Furthermore, school wastage promotes a 'culture of failure'. As said earlier (see Box 4), pupils who are unable to proceed with their classmates to the next grade frequently face problems of self-esteem and are likely to develop negative attitudes toward schooling. Repeaters thus become likely candidates for dropping out entirely.

Children's success in school is generally believed to be primarily a function of their innate intellectual aptitudes. Yet, in the case of pupils who come from deprived home environments, their living conditions may considerably reduce their motivation and opportunities to learn, whatever their intellectual ability may be. Also, the language of instruction may put certain children at a distinct disadvantage (see Box 6). By disregarding these conditions and attributing poor academic performance to the assumed 'inability' of the child, the school merely reinforces discriminatory social conditions.

Box 6. Speaking the Same Language

'Schooling that cuts the young child off from the home language is a major cause of drop-out and repetition', argues Joseph Poth of UNESCO's LINGUAPAX project. 'The language spoken in the family is best for the child's early learning. This fact must prevail over political and ideological considerations.' LINGUAPAX was established in 1986 to promote multi-lingual education and the respect of linguistic diversity. It elaborates guidelines for language policies in education, develops appropriate teaching materials for multilingual education and produces practical guides for use in training institutes.

Multilingual societies outnumber monolingual societies in the world and respecting linguistic diversity is no easy task. For example, there are some 1,200 recognized languages in India, using various systems of writing. In Papua New Guinea, there are roughly 600 local languages. Some 400 languages are spoken in Latin America, while Africa counts over 2,000.

UNESCO's report on the use of vernacular languages in education (1953) asserts the right of all children to be educated in their native tongue. But the practical difficulties of implementing that right are challenging and the question whether there can be a single 'language right' for all situations is a source of controversy. Governments in multilingual societies decide which languages are official—used by government, the media and the schools. This decision is often motivated by the political and social need to promote a lingua franca.

The choice of the language of instruction is important to students in several ways, since it can offer, or obstruct, access to a language of wide communication, which in turn can facilitate their access to information, humanity's cultural heritage, and job opportunities.

However, there is broad agreement among linguistic experts that pupils should learn to read in their native language and then transfer their reading skills to a second language. Several assessments of bilingual education programmes show that this approach contributes to better learning and reduces dropout and repetition. A landmark six-year primary education project using the Yoruba language in Nigeria found that "groups in the experimental classes obtained better results across the board... than the control groups". Similarly, the Institute of Educational Reform in Burkina Faso found that "expulsions and dropouts were practically nil... children were quick on the uptake" in experimental classes using local languages.

In Guatemala, where a national bilingual education programme was established in 1979 with support from USAID and the World Bank, the national curriculum was adapted and translated into four Mayan languages. Compared with a control group of Mayan children who were taught only in Spanish, the bilingual programme students had lower failure, repetition and dropout rates. They scored higher in comprehension and in all subjects, including Spanish, and their promotion rate was nine per cent higher. Parental support for the bilingual programme also led to an increased demand for education.

In multilingual contexts, the choice of what language to use in school should not be a question of 'either/or' but 'both'. Instruction in the mother tongue in the early grades followed by use of the official language, if different from the mother tongue, is now widely viewed as the most effective approach.

What Can be Done About School Wastage?

The causes of school wastage are multiple, but fall into two general categories: those that are rooted in the overall social and economic environment and those that stem from the way the school system itself is organised and operates. Social and economic forces are largely beyond the control of educators but may be influenced by public policies in areas such as transport, health services and labour laws. However, certain factors contributing to school wastage can be readily addressed by education officials.

Policies Related to Social and Economic Conditions

Data from UNESCO and other sources show that drop-out rates are highly sensitive to the national economic context. Studies in certain less developed countries, for example, have shown a significant and positive correlation between drop-out rates and the percentage of people living below the poverty line, i.e. on less than $1 a day (see *Figure 19*, Panel C).

Figure 19 shows that school wastage correlates also with several educational, social and demographic variables. For instance, as access to health services increases, so does the survival rate to Grade 5. As one would expect, children do better in school when they are healthy.

Countries with similar social indices sometimes report quite different patterns of repetition, while countries at quite different levels of development tend to have dissimilar levels of drop-out. It appears that drop-out rates are closely linked to the general state of a society—its level of economic and cultural development, how social services are distributed and attitudes toward education—while the repetition rates are largely determined by school policies.

Lowering the Costs of Schooling

Even when public schools are ostensibly free, parents must bear various direct costs to educate their children. Often, they must purchase school supplies and textbooks. While school uniforms may be a source of pride for pupils and their families, they can represent a major cost for parents with limited means. Developing countries frequently impose de facto tuition charges in the form of fees for registration, examinations and other services. In many cases these 'uses fees' total many times the amount the government's expenditure per pupil.

Fig. 19: Factors associated with internal efficiency of primary schooling in the less developed regions, around 1995

A. Higher pupil-teacher ratios correlate with lower school efficiency

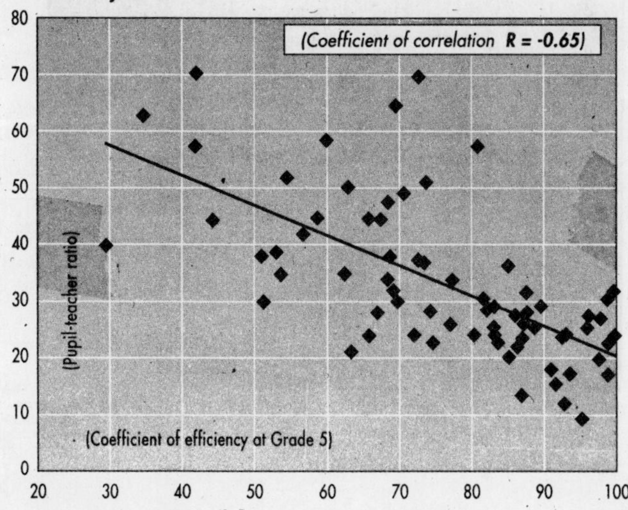

B. Lower percentage of repeaters correlate with higher survival rates

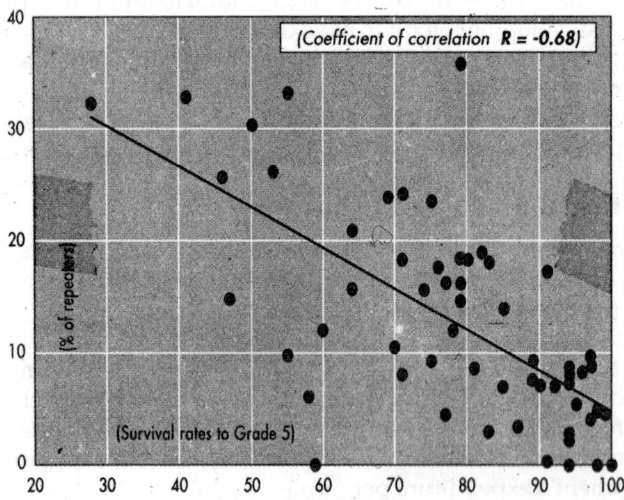

C. Higher drop-out rates correlate with more widespread poverty

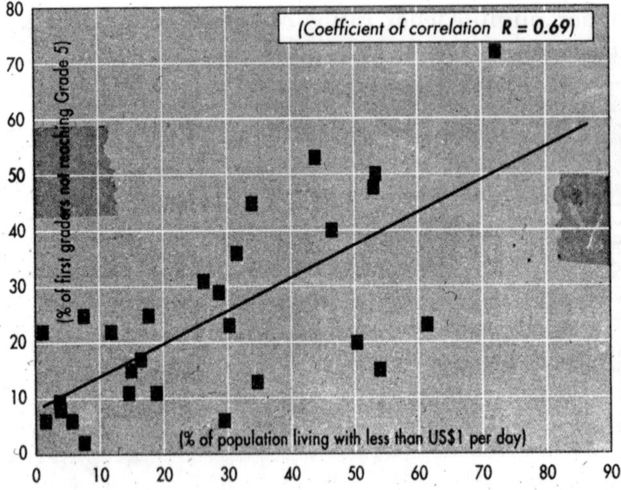

D. Lower survival rates correlate with higher proportions of the population in the 0-14 years-range

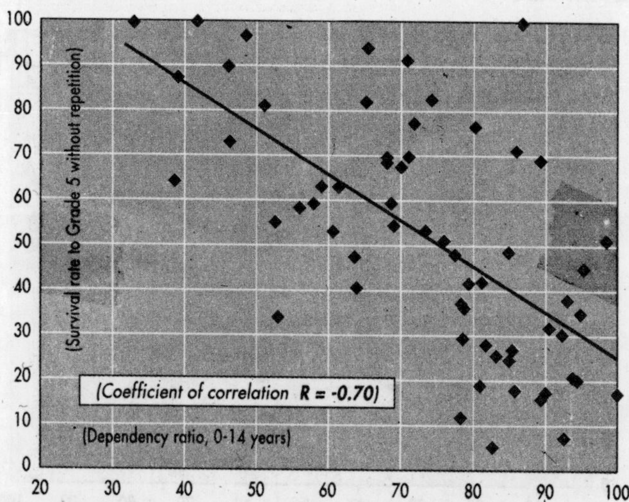

E. Higher school efficiency correlates with greater access to safe water

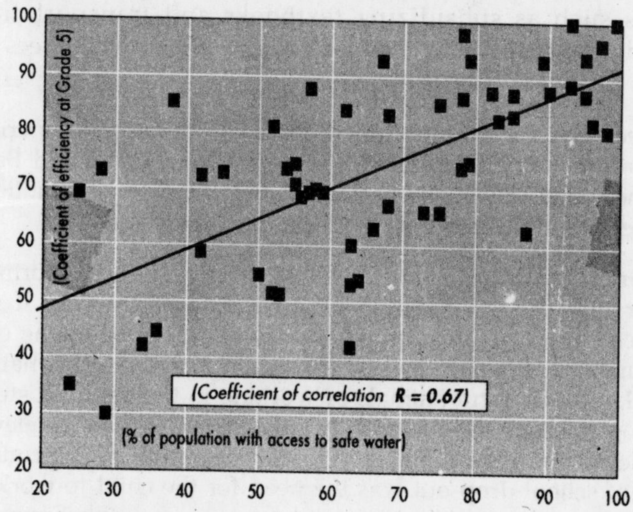

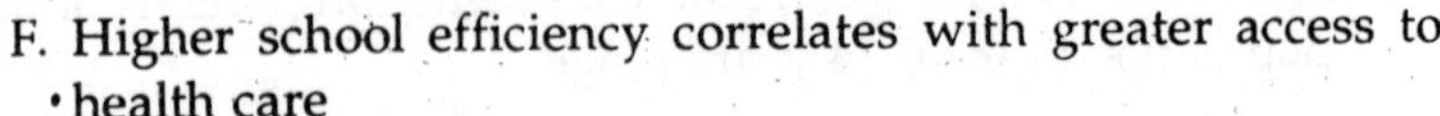

F. Higher school efficiency correlates with greater access to health care

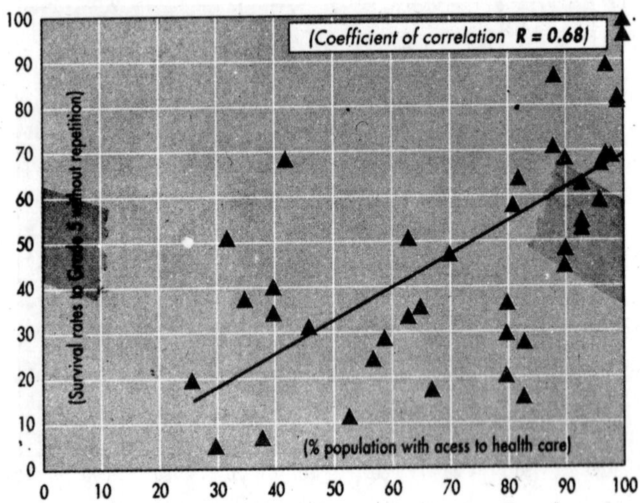

Public policy-makers can reduce these direct costs that families must bear to enrol their children in school through means such as subsidizing textbooks and transportation, providing essential school supplies and waiving school fees for pupils from very poor families.

Recently, for example, in response to the economic crisis, Indonesia obtained a rescue programme from the World Bank and the Asian Development Bank to help keep some 25 million Indonesian pupils in school over the next five years.

Families also face indirect costs, primarily in the form of labour that the child would otherwise be performing if not enrolled in school. Thus, pupils in school cannot be taking care of younger siblings in the home or selling goods in the market or looking after farm animals or working in the fields. A study of school wastage conducted in twenty-four schools in the eleven counties of the State of Bahia in Brazil showed that the primary cause of school-drop-out was the need for the child to work to help support the family. A report prepared for the Egyptian Ministry of Education in 1993 estimated that more than 1.5 million children under the age of 15 formed part of the working population.

Both the direct and indirect costs of schooling are particularly important in the case of girls. When poor families conclude that they can afford to educate only some of their children, they tend to favour sons over daughters in the belief that it is more important for boys to be equipped to enter the job market. In some countries, it is common for the eldest daughter to drop out of school as soon as there are younger brothers and sisters for her to look after and she is unlikely to return to school even if the younger, siblings, both male and female, enter school.

Improving Access to Schooling

Lack of proximity to schools is an important cause of wastage, especially for younger children in rural areas who need a school close to their homes. Some countries are overcoming this obstacle by setting up community schools or 'branch' or 'feeder' schools connected to established schools. Even though these small schools often can offer only the first few primary grades, they can have a positive impact on access, especially for girls. A UNESCO survey in 1991 showed that the proportion of incomplete schools in rural areas was over 30 per cent in nearly half of the countries of sub-Saharan Africa and in one-third of the Arab States and countries in the Latin America and Caribbean region.

However, the pupils who enter these incomplete schools often find it difficult to continue their schooling at a more distant location. If there is no provision of school transport or midday meals, only the most motivated families will continue sending their children to school away from the local community. A few countries, such as Bhutan, Malaysia and Thailand, are overcoming this difficulty by providing limited boarding facilities for pupils who live great distances from school, but this solution is more often used for post-primary levels of education.

Another approach to expanding access, used in the Philippines and Thailand, for example, is to employ 'mobile teachers' who travel by horseback or other means to reach pupils in remote areas. Yet another approach that is used in thinly populated areas is to permit teachers to teach several grades simultaneously—multigrade instruction. To be effective, this approach requires ample availability of teaching materials, since pupils must spend a good part of the school day working on their own or in small groups while the teacher is working with pupils in other 'grades'.

The provision of adequate classrooms and teachers in accessible schools is an important condition for universal primary education, but other, complementary measures have proved necessary to ensure that all children actually attend school. Parents need to be encouraged and convinced to send their children to school and compulsory education laws need to be enforced. Child labour laws that are in conformity with international standards and that are rigorously enforced tend to ensure that children are not kept out of school.

Box 7. Food for Thought

When some primary schools in the Ethiopian regions of Amhara and Tigray started to distribute food to their pupils in a project sponsored by the World Food Programme (WFP) enrolments increased by over 50 per cent between 1994 and 1995. Drop-out and attendance rates, along with performance in the end-of-year examinations, improved as well. And most of the new pupils had never been to school before.

The positive effects of school feeding programmes have been demonstrated in many other countries, too. In Morocco, for example, children were more likely to enrol and remain in schools with a canteen. A school feeding programme in Burkina Faso resulted in increased enrolments and less absenteeism and drop-out, as well as improvements in repetition and examination pass rates. In Benin, the existence of a school canteen was associated with higher learning achievement. By contrast, one-fourth of the pupils dropped out of school when a school feeding programme was interrupted in the Dominican Republic.

In poor communities, where the direct and indirect costs and poor quality of education lead parents to keep their children out of school, the distribution of school meals can be a strong incentive for children to enrol and attend regularly. Since absenteeism often leads to drop-out, encouraging regular attendance tends to prevent drop-out. Pupils who have attended school throughout the year are also more likely to succeed in examinations.

School feeding programmes are also often an effective way to involve parents in school affairs and improve school-community relations. For example, parent-teacher associations help run the school canteens in Côte d'Ivoire that receive food aid from WFP. When parents are motivated and involved in school life, the education of their children benefits.

The positive effects of school feeding on education can be enhanced even further if it is combined with other health and nutrition interventions for school children, such as de-worming and micro-nutrient supplementation.

Even well-nourished children have concentration problems when they are hungry. One study in Canada showed that low-achieving children ate breakfast less regularly than did high-achieving children from similar backgrounds. Short-term hunger has even more detrimental effects in undernourished children, especially if they walk long distances to school.

School feeding programmes, whether sponsored by food aid organisations or functioning with local resources, exist in most countries. When they are well organised, they can make an important contribution to reducing educational wastage.

Changing Educational Policies and Practices

Common sense suggests—and numerous studies have confirmed—that children are far more likely to be motivated to learn and to persist in school if the curricula and teaching methods are of high quality. By contrast, pupils who are bored and fail to see the connection between their personal lives and what they are taught in school become candidates for academic failure and, eventually, dropping out.

There is much that can and must be done to improve the quality of instruction through a concerted strategy to improve the curricula, the training of teachers and to reorganisation of the school to promote learning. The involvement and leadership of the school head can make or break any attempt at reform, as the experience of Chile's 900 Schools Programme shows. There, school directors and programme supervisors devise an annual improvement plan to examine their needs, raise their standards and, in co-operation with teachers, evaluate their work.

Improving Teaching Methods

Numerous studies have established that skilled teaching has a strong positive impact on pupil achievement. For example, a recent study in rural Pakistan found that investments that improve teacher quality and increase student exposure to teachers are likely to have higher returns in schooling effectiveness than those that improve physical infrastructure and equipment. Another recent large-scale research project in the United States found that the wide disparities in achievement between black and white pupils attending different schools were almost entirely accounted for by the qualifications of teachers.

But improving the quality of teacher training requires more than imparting new pedagogical techniques. Several surveys have shown that many teachers do not feel responsible in any way for their pupils' failures. Instead, they believe that learning abilities are innate, so they tend to ascribe failure primarily to a pupil's low intelligence, lack of work or family background. These teachers regard their task as merely transmitting knowledge, rather than guiding pupils through a learning process.

Such attitudes among teachers are often intensified by poor working conditions and the lack of any professional framework through which they could exchange experiences and learn from their peers. Also, teacher morale and salaries are low in many countries, which does not encourage them to seek to improve their skills.

Any systematic effort to reduce school wastage school include measures to enhance the skills and working conditions of classroom teachers, especially those who teach in the early grades where repetition is greatest. Both pre-service and in-service teacher training should aim to equip teachers with a variety of practical strategies for helping pupils learn in a timely fashion. Teachers need to master pupil-centred approaches that recognize that each pupil has specific learning needs and requires a particular set of interventions. Various strategies can be employed to upgrade teachers' skills and attitudes and their capacities to introduce new curricula materials and teaching methods.

Making Schools More Flexible

A number of countries, such as the Philippines, have found that school attendance can be improved and wastage reduced by organizing school calendars so that pupils in rural areas are not expected to attend school during planting and harvest seasons when their families need their labour. Similarly, the hours of the school day can be set to take account of the fact that some pupils, especially girls, must perform household chores.

Classes that include pupils of different ages have been found, under certain conditions, to be an effective way of dealing with the fact that pupils develop at different paces, especially during the primary school years. When teachers have been trained to manage such classes and to take advantage of the instructional possibilities inherent in such diversity, they often find that retention becomes unnecessary.

Early Intervention

A considerable body of literature demonstrates the advantages of 'front-loading' educational services to make sure that pupils get off to a good start in their schooling and build a strong base for future learning. A study in Madagascar, for instance, found strong correlations between pre-school education and lower school wastage rates. A study in Mexico estimated that pre-school education produced a 19 per cent improvement in performance on mathematics tests among the children of poor families.

In most developing countries, however, early childhood education is still considered to be a luxury and most such programmes are located in urban areas only. They are often considered by the personnel and the parents as a downward extension of schooling. Consequently, the personnel are not always sensitive to the developmental needs of pre-school children and force them prematurely into routine reading and writing.

Well-designed early childhood development programmes have proved to be effective in helping pupils from poor families to acquire some of the cultural attitudes and school-readiness skills that children from more affluent families learn in their homes. It is important, however, that such programmes be carried out by competent personnel with special training. Instructional methods should aim to awaken children's interest in learning rather than to push them to early acquisition of formal academic skills.

The high rate of repetition in Grade 1 suggests how important it is for pupils to get off to a good start in their schooling. The selection, competence and behaviour of teachers responsible for the entry grade should be a priority in efforts to combat wastage. School administrators would do well to assign the best teachers to work with the beginning pupils.

A number of countries have found ways to put more resources, including teaching time, into the early grades. One approach is to provide remedial measures for chronic repeaters. Brazil's State of Saõ Paolo, for example, has developed an anti-wastage strategy that consists of creating accelerated classes for repeaters at two levels (Grades 1 and 2 and Grades 3 and 4) with the aim of rapid promotion to the higher level. Intensive study in small groups and a belief in the pupils' innate possibilities are the hallmarks of this strategy, which targets the counties and schools with the biggest age-range per grade.

Inclusive Education

An estimated 10 per cent of all pupils have significant difficulties in learning at school. Children's disabilities and other learning difficulties may result from a number of factors: those within the child but also environmental factors such as poverty or lack of stimulation and school-related factors such as lack of good instructional materials, and inappropriate teaching and assessment standards. The very concept of 'special needs' has thus widened to include all children who are failing to benefit from school for whatever reasons. Special education is no longer a marginal issue and is now more commonly referred to as inclusive education or the 'one school for all' approach.

School teachers need to be prepared for this shift in approach through pre-service and in-service training. Certain prevalent attitudes towards disabilities also need to be reassessed so that schools can meet the learning needs of all the children in a community together.

Making Educational Materials More Available

Teaching aids, including textbooks, are scarce in many schools in developing countries. Faced with inadequate budgets that must cover teachers' salaries first, many ministries of education have little funding left to spend on textbooks and supplies. Yet numerous studies have demonstrated that the availability of textbooks is one of the major contributors to effective learning.

A 1997 UNESCO study on sustainable book provision points out that only a handful of industrialized nations possess both the technology of publishing and the knowledge and research to sustain a publishing industry. With few exceptions, developing countries, are poorly equipped to produce good quality learning materials. Consequently, they continue to import textbooks, but often in too small quantities, which is a costly way to alleviate some of the symptoms, rather than deal with the source of the problem—the absence of a publishing industry of their own. Even when educators in these countries develop suitable educational materials, they often do so with little awareness of the professional skills needed to publish and distribute books at a reasonable cost.

The promotion of national publishing industries is a promising strategy to enable countries to produce and disseminate suitable learning materials for their schools, as well as to more towards the wider goal of education for all, by creating and supporting a culture of reading.

Closing the Gender Gap

Last but not least, attaining the goal of Education for All requires overcoming the gender gap in primary schooling that characterizes most developing countries. To do so, it is necessary to understand the causes of the gap.

Box 8. Starting Early in the Caribbean

'We are Servol, and we care' says a charter written by the staff. Born in the aftermath of a social explosion in 1970, Servol (Service Volunteered for All) defined its programmes by listening to the marginalized and disadvantaged people in the slums of Laventille, Trinidad and Tobago. The outcome was two successful community-based programmes: early childhood centres for 2-5 year-olds and skills-training centres for teenage drop-outs. 'Each centre has to be run by the local community', says executive director Sister Ruth Montrichard, who describes Servol's work as 'respectful intervention in the lives of others'.

The 4,500 pre-school children who pass through Servol's 148 early childhood centres each year are well prepared for the demands of primary school. Teachers help children develop physically, intellectually, creatively, emotionally and spiritually rather than pressure them into reading and writing and counting at an early age. The curriculum is geared to learning about the Caribbean heritage: children make masks, costumes and instruments for Carnival, and they colour flags on Independence Day. The children are introduced to art, drama, music and dance. Intellectual activities involve concepts of time, space, language, colours and pre-writing skills.

Programme evaluations in 1990 and 1995 noted that pupils entering primary school from Servol pre-schools tended to be more sociable, speak up in class and generally communicate more than the other children, even those who attended other pre-schools.

Servol's pre-school teacher training course is recognized by Oxford University. Candidates selected from 15 Caribbean territories spend one year full-time in the Port-of-Spain training centre and a one-year internship in the field, during which they are regularly monitored. Besides administering its 188 centres in Trinidad and Tobago, Servol monitors a similar number in 15 other Caribbean territories.

Recognizing that parents are the primary care-givers, Servol also trains para-professionals to go from village to village educating parents. They explain how harsh discipline or neglect stunts a child's potential. The child's emotional needs, nutrition, hygiene and environmental issues are also addressed. Teenage parents have been particularly responsive. The pre-school teachers have noted that increased parental awareness produces results such as improved cleanliness, punctuality and attendance among the children and more nutritious food and fewer sweets in their lunch-boxes.

The world children have to face is tough and competitive. To survive, according to Servol, children must have a well-developed personality. Its pre-schools help young children to develop a positive self-image, to be resourceful and curious about learning, and to be responsible and caring towards the world around them. Servol believes that empowerment at the grassroots is the most effective tool for building a nation and it has convincingly demonstrated through its programmes that the vicious cycle of poverty, violence and despair can be broken.

Box 9. The Parent Factor

In a survey conducted in China, primary school drop-outs were asked: 'Under what circumstances would you not have dropped out of school?' Nearly one out of three responded: 'If my parents had given more support, I would not have dropped out'. The same survey revealed that nearly half (47.1 per cent) of the primary-school drop-outs left school at the decision of their parents.

Governments in many countries, including China, have used massive publicity campaigns to increase public awareness of the economic and other benefits of education and to convince parents to enrol and keep their children in school. Such campaigns have been particularly successful in raising enrolment and survival rates among girls. Campaigns make use of radio, television and videos as well as low tech means such as posters and street theatre. They are most effective when they have the support of political, religious and other leaders in the country and when they are carried out in partnership with women's groups and civic organisations.

Such information campaigns generally encourage parents to enrol their children promptly when they reach the entry age of compulsory schooling. This not only benefits the children but makes the teachers' work easier because they can deal with a narrower age range among their pupils. Some campaigns seek also to sensitize policy-makers to the causes of school wastage and its harmful effects, and then to build their commitment to adopt solutions.

The impact of parents' education on the schooling of children is well documented. In many countries, the educational level of parents is the single best predictor of how long children will stay in school and how well they will perform scholastically. Programmes that promote literacy among parents are thus likely to have positive educational effects on their children as well. Such programmes, often target recent school drop-outs, female heads of households and young women in the 16 to 25 age-group, who are most likely to have young children.

Most societies make a clear distinction between men's roles and women's roles, and the latter often lie outside the mainstream of economic activities. One result, especially in rural communities, is that the education of girls is considered less important than the education of boys. Where the practice of child marriage continues, girls are withdrawn from school at puberty or are never enrolled. A study in Sierra Leone on the impact of the economic crisis on girls' education showed that parents chose to cut costs by withdrawing daughters before sons from the school.

With few exceptions, boys tend to be enrolled in school at significantly higher rates than girls in all developing regions and they then complete the primary-school cycle in larger numbers, see *Figure 20*. However, a closer look at the data shows that once girls are admitted to school, their drop-out rate is no higher than that for boys. This suggests that strategies to remove the gender gap should concentrate on getting more girls into school in the first place.

Various measures have proved effective in increasing girls' enrolment, such as waiving or reducing school fees for girls, supplying free textbooks, providing stipends for girls, offering flexible school hours and establishing childcare centres for the young siblings of girl pupils. To encourage the enrolment of girls, programmes in Pakistan and Niger give girl pupils a take-home food ration. Such incentives tend to encourage regular attendance and reduce drop-out. In some cultures, the location of schools and their physical facilities influence girls' access to education. Building schools close to girls' homes, providing separate sanitary facilities and constructing boundary walls can encourage parents to sent their daughters to school.

Some countries have found that girls' enrolment and performance improve if they can attend single-sex, schools. Bangladesh, Chad, India, Pakistan, Senegal and Yemen have made special efforts to build new classrooms for girls. (See also Box 10, Girl-friendly schools in Egypt). Similarly, in some rural areas and traditional communities, girls' enrolment tends to increase when there are women teachers in the school.

In the long term, education itself can help close the gender gap. Curricula that convey positive images of girls and women contribute to removing gender biases and harmful attitudes towards women. Educated women are better equipped to exercise their rights and educated men are more considerate and ready to regard women as equals. Enlightened public policy can hasten reaching a critical mass of educated men and women who truly understand the importance of educating their sons...and daughters.

Box 10. Girl-Friendly Schools in Egypt

We wish all girls, women and men in our village could get an education, but we cannot afford it, nor can we allow girls to walk long distances on their own.

An elderly man in rural Egypt

In Egypt, some 4.2 million children don't go to school, and their ranks grow yearly by some 350,000 more who reach school age but fail to enrol or who drop out. Among adults, only about a third of Egyptian women are literate, compared to about two-thirds of Egyptian men. This disparity is even more marked in rural areas, notably in Upper Egypt.

While over half the boys from isolated hamlets walk to the nearest government primary school, most of the girls do not because of their parents' fears or because of the hidden costs of 'free' primary education. Poor families who cannot afford to educate all of their children tend to favour the sons, so that in many hamlets, not even 15 per cent of the girls go to school.

The Community School Project began when the Ministry of Education, realizing that innovative measures were needed to provide universal primary schooling by the year 2000, asked UNICEF to design a pilot school project that would use non-conventional means to remove the regional and gender disparities marring Egypt's report card. The involvement of the communities themselves was a priority consideration for the project's developers. While scouting for sites, they found a strong desire for girls' education, so long as it was provided in the community.

The first four schools in a rural district were an immediate success. In what became standard procedure, the local families supplied a schoolroom close to their homes and formed a committee to manage the school and ensure regular attendance. Schooling was completely free, with no costs for uniforms or books.

Eliminating the long walk to school is a crucial girl-friendly feature. So is recruiting young local women to be trained as 'facilitators' (para-professional teachers) who organize activities, provide materials and stimulate children's learning, rather than 'delivering knowledge'.

By the end of 1997, the project was so successful that 151 community schools were operating in some of the most conservative areas of Egypt, with girls making up 70 per cent of the pupils. The plan is to have 50 more schools in operation by 1999.

The schools are inviting, lively places decorated with the pupils' artwork. A child-centred approach is used, with songs, games and stories relating to the children's daily lives. To facilitators and children collect and use odds and ends from bottle caps to toothbrushes as teaching and learning aids. Although the daily timetable allows children to carry out their agricultural or domestic chores at home, the syllabus provides the equivalent of a full primary school programme, covering Arabic, religious studies, arithmetic, local history, science and art. Children also acquire life skills such as problem-solving and civic behaviour, and learn about health and the environment.

The community provides the school premises and the Ministry of Education finances the facilitators' salaries, training and books. UNICEF trains the facilitators, furnishes the classrooms and supports local organisations that implement the project.

The community schools have acted as a catalyst for other development activities. In 1995, about 1,600 women attended literacy classes in the schools. Health posts, water and sanitation supplies, and income-generating activities have grown up around them. Their success has not escaped the attention of Egypt's decision-makers: the Ministry of Education has announced its intention to open some 3,000 one-classroom schools in rural areas, similar to the community schools, and under the patronage of First Lady Mrs. Mubarak.

Retention Versus Automatic Promotion

Whereas drop-out rates are often affected by social and economic forces beyond the control of educators, decisions on whether or not to promote pupils to the next grade are generally made by teachers. Repetition rates are thus a matter of educational policy and practice.

Unfortunately, decisions on repetition are sometimes taken for reasons that have little to do with the presumed educational benefits. A study on school wastage in Bahia, Brazil, found that such decisions are often made by teachers in a haphazard and discriminatory manner. Considerations such as dress codes, speech and social status frequently entered the picture. In other cases, retention—and even expulsion—were used to punish pupils considered to be inattentive, or insufficiently motivated or otherwise unco-operative.

In formulating promotion policies, school authorities would be well advised to survey the research literature first. A significant body of research indicates that the negative effects of repetition largely outstrip the expected benefits. One study by the International Association for the Evaluation of Educational Achievement, for example, found no absolute relation between retention policies and overall pupil achievement. It noted that pupils in the Scandinavian countries and Japan, which have done away with grade repetition, typically perform well above the international average on comperative examinations.

However, it should also be noted that several countries that at one time or another had policies of automatic promotion later abandoned them. Panama and Puerto Rico decided to do away with automatic promotion when they discovered that too many pupils were leaving school lacking sufficient skills. Moreover, opposition to automatic promotion is strong among members of the teaching profession who, like most people, are reluctant to give up practices that have been followed for many years. This opposition is sometimes reinforced by broken promises of additional resources for remedial measures to help pupils promoted automatically despite their scholastic under-achievement.

Moreover, evaluation of pupils' achievement should be continuous, with the aim of detecting and compensating learning difficulties rather than selecting pupils for promotion. In Malaysia, for example, where automatic promotion is practised in the nine grades of primary and lower secondary education, each school assesses the achievement of its own pupils. There is also a national test each year for pupils in Grades 3 and 5, the results of which help teachers to make a better evaluation of their pupils' achievement and to compare it with the performance of pupils in other schools.

Some countries have taken a compromise position and permit repeating only at certain strategic points in a child's education.

Fig. 20: Out-of-school primary-school-age children in the less developed regions, by gender, 1985 and 1995 (in thousands).

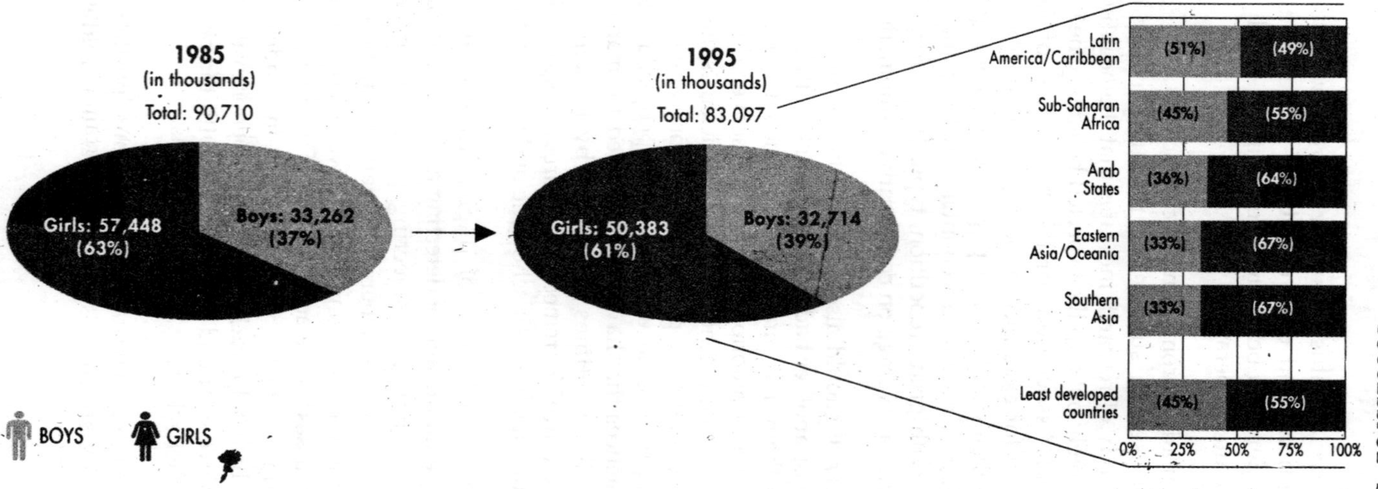

For example, Botswana allows repetition only for Grade 4 pupils who do not score sufficiently high on an achievement test and for Grade 7 pupils who do not gain admission to secondary school.

It is important to recognize that neither automatic promotion nor retention policies, by themselves, can solve the problems of children who experience difficulty in learning. Pupils who move on to the next grade without having mastered material at the previous level are likely to have trouble learning the new subject matter, too. Pupils who fail to grasp material presented in a particular manner and setting are not likely to have much more success by going through an identical experience a second time. In both cases, the more effective approach would be to provide specific teaching interventions that address the particular learning needs of each pupil.

Conclusion

There is no universal set of solutions to the problems of school wastage. Educators and policy-makers need first to identify the predominant causes of drop-out and repetition in their particular situation and then devise appropriate solutions, which may need to target particular grades, geographical areas, communities, and disadvantaged groups. Such decisions will be more soundly based when a suitable data collection system is in place, which can then provide feed-back once the corrective measures are under way.

Any attempt to reduce school wastage must be comprehensive and systematic in order to deal with its multiple causes. Some aspects of wastage, notably high repetition rates, can be addressed through changes in educational practice that are largely under the control of educational policy-makers. Other components, such as dropping out, are rooted mainly in economic and social conditions external to the school. Addressing them requires working with members of local communities as well as with political and other leaders. It is thus incumbent upon teachers and school administrators to make their fellow citizens aware of the cost to families and to society when children are excluded from school or fail in school.

A review of the research on grade repetition, provides no conclusive evidence to support the hypothesis that repetition is a more effective way of helping low achievers than automatic promotion. As repeaters use resources that could otherwise be used to expand enrolment or to improve the quality of educational services, countries with high levels of repetition should review their promotion policies with a view to adopting more efficient measures to improve learning achievement and prevent failure. The elimination of drop-out and repetition, however, would not necessarily solve the problem of under-achievement. Pupil-centred instruction and various other pedagogical improvements can raise the learning achievement of all pupils and thereby increase the efficiency of primary education.

Bibliography

Behrman, J.; et al. School Quality and Cognitive Achievement Production: A Case Study for Rural Pakistan. *Economics of Education Review*, Vol. 16, 1997. pp. 127-42.

Darling-Hammond, L.; Falk, B. Using Standards to Support Student Learning. *Phi Delta Kappan*, November 1997.

Fiske, E. B. *Using Both Hands, Women and Education in Cambodia*, Manila, Asian Development Bank Queensland Education Consortium, 1995.

Fafunwa, A.B. Using National Languages in Education: A Challenge to African Educators. In: *African Thoughts on the Prospects of Education for All*, pp. 97-110 Dakar, UNESCO/UNICEF, 1990.

International Labour Organisation's Home web page, http://www.ilo.org, March 1998.

Landers, C. *Language Rights in Early Childhood Care and Development*, from Early Childhood Care and Development web site, http://www.ecdgroup.com.

Meeting on Strategies to Reduce Wastage and Increase Efficiency in Education, 18 October—7 November 1990, Tokyo. *Regional Study of Wastage in Education: Reducing Wastage and Increasing Efficiency in Education—Problems, Causes, Strategies and Programmes*. Tokyo, UNESCO/APEID/NIERI, 1990.

Miller del Rosso, J.; Marek, T. *Class Action. Improving School Performance in the Developing World Through Better Health and Nutrition. Directions in Development*, Washington D.C., The World Bank. 1996.

Morocco, Ministère de l'éducation nationale. *Analyse Des Déterminants De La Scolarisation En Zone Rurale Au Maroc.* Dijon, 1993. (Study Carried Out in Collaboration with IREDU-CNRS).

Pollit, E. *Malnutrition and Infection in the Classroom*. Paris, UNESCO, 1990.

Primary School Repetition: A Global Perspective, Geneva, International Bureau of Education/UNICEF, 1996.

Priorities and Strategies for Education. A World Bank Review, Washington D.C., The World Bank, 1995.

Sanou, F. Who's Afraid of National Languages as Instructional Media and Why? In: *African Thoughts on the Prospects of Education for All*, pp. 75-96 Dakar, UNESCO/UNICEF, 1990.

Synthesis of Research on School Readiness and Kindergarten Retention. *Educational Leadership*, November 1986, p. 86.

Turning Points: Preparing American Youth for the 21st Century. Report of the Task Force on Education of Young Adolescents. 1989.

Universal Declaration of Human Rights, New York, United Nations. Internet: www.un.org/overview/rights.html.

Vaznaugh, A. *Dropout Intervention and Language Minority Youth.* Centre for Applied Linguistics, ERIC Digest, 1995. From web site, http://www.cal.org.

World Conference on Education for All, Meeting Basic Learning Needs, Jomtien, Thailand, 1990. *World Declaration on Education for All and Framework for Action to Meet Basic Learning Needs.* Third Printing Paris, UNESCO for the Secretariat of the EFA Forum, 1994.

World Education Report 1995, Paris, UNESCO Publishing, 1995.

World Education Report 1998, Paris, UNESCO Publishing, 1998.

Additional Reading

Bhaskara Rao, Digumarti (1994). *Scientific Aptitude*. New Delhi: Ashish Publishing House. ISBN 81-7024-658-X.

Bhaskara Rao, Digumarti (1995). *Animal Kingdom*. New Delhi: Discovery Publishing House. ISBN 81-7141-274-2.

Bhaskara Rao, Digumarti (1995). *Batracology*. New Delhi: Discovery Publishing House. ISBN 81-7141-279-3.

Bhaskara Rao, Digumarti (1996). *Scientific Attitude vis-a-vis Scientific Aptitude*. New Delhi: Discovery Publishing House. ISBN 81-7141-308-0.

Bhaskara Rao, Digumarti, ed. (1996). *Encyclopaedia of Education For All*. 5 Vols. New Delhi: APH Publishing Corporation. ISBN 81-7024-759-4. (Set).

Vol. I Education For All: The World Conference. ISBN 81-7024-760-8.

Vol. II Education For All: The EPA-9 Summit. ISBN 81-7024-761-6.

Vol. III Education For All: Quality Education For All. ISBN 81-7024-762-4.

Vol.IV Education For All: Planning and Monitoring. ISBN 81-7024-763-2.

Vol.V Education For All: The Indian Scenario. ISBN 81-7024-764-0.

Bhaskara Rao, Digumarti, ed. (1996). *Global Perceptions on Peace Education*, 3 Vols. New Delhi: Discovery Publishing House.ISBN 81-7141-319-6.

Bhaskara Rao, Digumarti, ed. (1996). *National Policy on Education*, 2 Vols. New Delhi: Anmol Publications Pvt. Ltd. ISBN 81-7488-323-1.

Bhaskara Rao, Digumarti, ed. (1997). *Care the Child*, 2 Vols. New Delhi: Discovery Publishing House. ISBN 81-7141-394-3.

Bhaskara Rao, Digumarti, ed. (1997). *Education for the 21st Century*. New Delhi: Discovery Publishing House. ISBN 81-7141-389-7.

Bhaskara Rao, Digumarti, ed. (1997). *Reflections on Scientific Attitude*. New Delhi: Discovery Publishing House. ISBN 81-7141-328-5.

Bhaskara Rao, Digumarti (1997). *Scientific Attitude*. New Delhi: Discovery Publishing House. ISBN 81-7141-381-1.

Bhaskara Rao, Digumarti, ed. (1997). *Success Story of a Primary Education Project*. New Delhi: APH Publishing Corporation. ISBN 81-7024-850-7.

Bhaskara Rao, Digumarti, ed. (1997). *World Food Summit*. New Delhi: Discovery Publishing House. ISBN 81-7141-386-2.

Bhaskara Rao, Digumarti, ed. (1998). *Adolescence Education*. New Delhi: Discovery Publishing House. ISBN 81-7141-432-X.

Bhaskara Rao, Digumarti, ed. (1998). *Community and School Nutrition Education*. New Delhi: Discovery Publishing House. ISBN 81-7141-435-4.

Bhaskara Rao, Digumarti, ed. (1998). *District Primary Education Programme*. New Delhi: Discovery Publishing House. ISBN 81-7141-396-X.

Bhaskara Rao, Digumarti, ed. (1998). *Earth Sunnnit*, 2 Vols. New Delhi: Discovery Publishing House. ISBN 81-7141-435-4.

Bhaskara Rao, Digumarti, ed. (1998). *National Policy on Education: Towards an Enlightened and Humane Society*. New Delhi: Discovery Publishing House. ISBN 81-7141-426-5.

Bhaskara Rao, Digumarti, ed. (1998). *Reforming School Education*. New Delhi: Discovery Publishing House. ISBN 81-7141-403-6.

Bhaskara Rao, Digumarti, ed. (1998). *Teacher Education in India*. New Delhi: Discovery Publishing House. ISBN 81-7141-406-0.

Bhaskara Rao, Digumarti, ed. (1998). *World Summit for Social Development*. New Delhi: Discovery Publishing House. ISBN 81-7141-420-6.

Bhaskara Rao, Digumarti, ed. (2000). *Education For All: Achieving the Goal*. 3 Vols. New Delhi: APH Publishing Corporation. ISBN 81-7648-152-1.

Vol. I The Global Consensus. ISBN 81-7648-153-X.

Vol. II Mid-Decade Review Reports of Regional Seminars. ISBN 81-7648-154-8.

Vol. III Issues and Trends. ISBN 81-7648-155-6.

Bhaskara Rao, Digumarti, ed. (2000). *International Encyclopaedia of AIDS*, 11 Vols in 13 Parts. New Delhi: Discovery Publishing House. ISBN 81-7141-465-6 (Set).

Vol. 1 Introduction to HIV/AIDS. ISBN 81-7141-523-7.

Vol. 2 HIV/AIDS—Issues and Challenges, 2 Parts. ISBN 81-7141-524-5.

Vol. 3 HIV/AIDS—Socio Economic Realities. ISBN 81-7141-525-3.

Vol. 4 HIV/AIDS Law Ethics and Human Rights, 2 Parts. ISBN 81-7141-526-1.

Vol. 5 AIDS and NGOs. ISBN 81-7141-527-X.

Vol. 6 AIDS and Home Care. ISBN 81-7141-528-8.

Vol. 7 STD Case Management. ISBN 81-7141-529-6.

Vol. 8 HIV Prevention and Care—Teaching Modules for Nurses and Midwives. ISBN 81-7141-530-X.

Vol. 9 HIV/AIDS Prevention Education for Educational Institutions. ISBN 81-7141-531-8.

Vol. 10 Instructional Modules for AIDS Education. ISBN 81-7141-532-6.

Vol. 11 School Health Education to Prevent AIDS and STD—A Package for Curriculum Planners. ISBN 81-7141-533-4.

Bhaskara Rao, Digumarti, ed. (2000). *International Encyclopaedia of Science and Technology Education*. 11 Volumes. New Delhi: Discovery Publishing House. ISBN 81-7141-548-2. (Set).

Vol. 1 Science and Technology Education. ISBN 81-7141-568-7.

Vol. 2 Science Education in Developing Countries. ISBN 81-7141-570-9.

Vol. 3 Organisational Structure of Science. ISBN 81-7141-570-9.

Vol. 4 Science Education in Asia and the Pacific. ISBN 81-7141-571-7.

Vol. 5 Science and Technology Education for All. ISBN 81-7141-572-5.

Vol. 6 Values, Ethics, Talent and Girls in Science and Technology Education. ISBN 81-7141-573-3.

Vol. 7 Popularization of Science and Technology Education. ISBN 81-7141-574-1.

Vol. 8 Science, Power and Society. ISBN 81-7141-575-X.

Vol. 9 Information Technology. ISBN 81-7141-576-8.

Vol. 10. Teacher Training in Science and Technology Education. ISBN 81-7141-577-6.

Vol. 11 Science, Technology and Society: A Curriculum Framework. ISBN 81-7141-578-4.

Bhaskara Rao, Digumarti, ed. (2001). *Distance Education in Different Countries*. New Delhi: APH Publishing Corporation. ISBN 81-7648-229-3.

Bhaskara Rao, Digumarti, ed. (2001). *Decentralised Management of Education (Management of Education in Panchayati Raj and Municipal Bodies)*. New Delhi: Discovery Publishing House. ISBN 81-7141-617-9.

Bhaskara Rao, Digumarti, ed. (2001). *Electrochemistry for Environmental Protection*. New Delhi: Discovery Publishing House. ISBN 81-7141-619-5.

Bhaskara Rao, Digumarti, ed. (2001). *Global Educational Studies*. New Delhi: Discovery Publishing House. ISBN 81-7141-616-0.

Bhaskara Rao, Digumarti, ed. (2001). *Global Synthesis of Educational Assessment*. New Delhi: Discovery Publishing House. ISBN 81-7141-613-6.

Bhaskara Rao, Digumarti, ed. (2001). *International Encyclopaedia of Human Rights*, 7 Volumes in 13 Parts. New Delhi: Discovery Publishing House. ISBN 81-7141-567-9 (Set).

Vol. 1 International Instruments of Human Rights, 2 Parts. ISBN 81-7141-595-4.

Vol. 2 Regional Instruments of Human Rights. ISBN 81-7141-604-7.

Vol. 3 Human Rights and The United Nations, 2 Parts. ISBN 81-7141-605-5.

Vol. 4 Fact Files of Human Rights, 2 Parts. ISBN 81-7141-606-3.

Vol. 5 Study Stories of Human Rights, 3 Parts. ISBN 81-7141-607-1.

Vol. 6 International Meetings on Human Rights, 2 Parts. ISBN 81-7141-608-X.

Vol. 7 Professional Training in Human Rights. ISBN 81-7141-609-8.

Bhaskara Rao, Digumarti, ed. (2001). *Jomtein Decade of Education*. New Delhi: Discovery Publishing House. ISBN 81-7141-618-7.

Bhaskara Rao, Digumarti, ed. (2001). *Nuclear Materials: Issues and Concerns*, 2 Vols. New Delhi: Discovery Publishing House. ISBN 81-7141-611-X.

Bhaskara Rao, Digumarti, ed. (2001). *World Conference on Education for All*. New Delhi: APH Publishing Corporation. ISBN 81-7648-274-9.

Bhaskara Rao, Digumarti, ed. (2001). *World Conference on Higher Education*. New Delhi: Discovery Publishing House. ISBN 81-7141-610-1.

Bhaskara Rao, Digumarti, ed. (2001). *World Conference on Science*. New Delhi: Discovery Publishing House. ISBN 81-7141-612-8.

Bhaskara Rao, Digumarti, ed. (2003). *Chernobyl: Never Again*. New Delhi: Discovery Publishing House.

Bhaskara Rao, Digumarti, ed. (2003). *Habitat Agenda*. New Delhi: Discovery Publishing House.

Bhaskara Rao, Digumarti, ed. (2002). *Inspiring Experiences in Teacher Education*. New Delhi: Discovery Publishing House.

Bhaskara Rao, Digumarti, ed. (2002). *International Studies in Education*. New Delhi: Discovery Publishing House. ISBN 81-7141-643-8.

Bhaskara Rao, Digumarti, ed. (2002). *Military Conversion: Impact on Science and Technology*. New Delhi: Discovery Publishing House. ISBN 81-7141-643-8.

Bhaskara Rao, Digumarti, ed. (2003). *Virology and Immunology*. New Delhi: Discovery Publishing House.

Bhaskara Rao, Digumarti, ed. (2002). *United Nations Millenium Summit*. New Delhi: Discovery Publishing House. ISBN 81-7141-632-2.

Bhaskara Rao, Digumarti, ed, (2002). *World Assembly on Aging*. New Delhi: Discovery Publishing House. ISBN 81-7141-637-3.

Bhaskara Rao, Digumarti, ed. (2003). *World Conference on Human Rights*. New Delhi: Discovery Publishing House.

Bhaskara Rao, Digumarti, ed. (2002). *World Education Forum*. New Delhi: Discovery Publishing House.

Bhaskara Rao, Digumarti, ed. (2003). *Education Employment and Human Resource Development*. New Delhi: Discovery Publishing House.

Bhaskara Rao, Digumarti, ed. (2003). *Educational Innovations in Action*. New Delhi: Discovery Publishing House.

Bhaskara Rao, Digumrati, ed. (2003). *Learning to Live Together*, 3 Volumes. New Delhi: Discovery Publishing House.

Bhaskara Rao, Digumarti, C.A.P. Swamy and B.S.V. Dutt (1997). *Self Evaluation in Student Teaching*. New Delhi: Discovery Publishing House. ISBN 81-7141-374-9.

Bhaskara Rao, Digumarti, C. Sridevi and K. Vijaya (1995). *Achievement in Social Studies*. New Delhi: Discovery Publishing House. ISBN 81-7141-281-5.

Bhaskara Rao, Digumarti and Digumarti Pushpa Latha (1994). *Achievement in Biology*. New Delhi: Discovery Publishing House. ISBN 81-7141-264-5.

Bhaskara Rao, Digumarti and Digumarti Pushpa Latha (1995). *Achievement in English*. New Delhi: Discovery Publishing House. ISBN 81-7141-283-1.

Bhaskara Rao, Digumarti and Digumarti Pushpa Latha (1995). *Achievement in Science*. New Delhi: Discovery Publishing House. ISBN 81-7141-280-7.

Bhaskara Rao, Digumarti and Digumarti Pushpa Latha (1995). *Achievement in Mathematics*. New Delhi: Discovery Publishing House. ISBN 81-7141-278-5.

Bhaskara Rao, Digumarti and Digumarti Pushpa Latha, eds. (1998). *International Encyclopaedia of Women*, 5 Vols. New Delhi: Discovery Publishing House. ISBN 81-7141-410-9.

Vol. 1 Status of World's Women. ISBN 81-7141-494-X.

Vol. 2 Women, Education and Empowerment. ISBN 81-7141-498-2.

Vol. 3 Women Challenges and Advancement. ISBN 81-7141-497-4.

Vol. 4 Women and Family Health. ISBN 81-7141-497-4.

Vol. 5 Women and International Action. ISBN 81-7141-498-2.

Bhaskara Rao, Digumarti, Digumarti Pushpa Latha and Digumarti Harshitha, eds. (2001). *Biological Warfare*. New Delhi: Discovery Publishing House. ISBN 81-7141-597-0.

Bhaskara Rao, Digumarti, Digumatri Pushpa Latha and Digumarti Harshitha, eds. (2001). *Women as Educators*. New Delhi: Discovery Publishing House. ISBN 81-7141-602-0.

Bhaskara Rao, Digumarti and Digumarti Harshitha, eds. (2000). *Education in India*. New Delhi: APH Publishing Corporation. ISBN 81-7648-207-2.

Bhaskara Rao, Digumarti, and Digumarti Harshitha, eds. (2001). *Assessing Learning Achievement*. New Delhi: Discovery Publishing House. ISBN 81-7141-601-2.

Bhaskara Rao, Digumarti and Digumarti Harshita, eds. (2001). *Energy Security*. New Delhi: Discovery Publishing House. ISBN 81-7141-598-9.

Bhaskara Rao, Digumarti, D. Harshitha and K.R.S.S. Rao, eds. (1999). *Advanced Biotechnology*. New Delhi: Discovery Publishing House. ISBN 81-7141-516-4.

Bhaskara Rao, Digumarti and D. Sridhar (2002). *Job Satisfaction of School Teachers*. New Delhi: Discovery Publishing House.

Bhaskara Rao, Digumarti and K.R.S. Sambasiva Rao, eds. (1996). *Current Trends in Indian Education*. New Delhi: Discovery Publishing House. ISBN 81-7141-311-0.

Bhaskara Rao, Digumarti and K. Vijaya (1995). *A Text Book Evaluation*. Ambala Cantt: The Associated Publishers.

Bhaskara Rao, Digumarti and N.V.M. Mohana Rao (2003). *Problems of Mentally Handicapped*. New Delhi: Discovery Publishing House.

Bhaskara Rao, Digumarti, V.V. Rao, V.V. Lakshmi and V.V. Krishna, eds. (2000). *Status and Advancement of Women*. New Delhi: APH Publishing Corporation. ISBN 81-7648-169-6.

Babu, P.C. and Digumarti Bhaskara Rao, ed. (2003). *Flowers of Wisdom*. New Delhi: Discovery Publishing House.

Bhagya Lakshmi, Lingineni and Digumarti Bhaskara Rao, ed. (2000). *Reading and Comprehension*. New Delhi: Discovery Publishing House. ISBN 81-7141-543-1.

Bhuvaneswara Lakshmi, G. and Digumarti Bhaskara Rao, ed. (2000). *Attitude Towards Science*. New Delhi: Discovery Publishing House. ISBN 81-7141-541-6.

Devraj, T.A.S. and Digumarti Bhaskara Rao, ed. (1997). *Trace Analysis of Uranium and Thorium*. New Delhi: Discovery Publishing House. ISBN 81-7141-375-7.

Durgani Rani, K. and Digumarti Bhaskara Rao, ed. (2000). *Educational Aspirations and Scientific Attitudes*. New Delhi: Discovery Publishing House. ISBN 81-7141-555-55.

Dutt, B.S.V. and Digumarti Bhaskara Rao (2001). *Empowering Primary Teachers*. New Delhi: Discovery Publishing House. ISBN 81-7141-615-2.

Ediger, Marlow and Digumarti Bhaskara Rao (1996). *Science Curriculum*. New Delhi: Discovery Publishing House. ISBN 81-7141-321-8.

Ediger, Marlow and Digumarti Bhaskara Rao (2000). *Teaching Mathematics Successfully*. New Delhi: Discovery Publishing House. ISBN 81-7141-552-0.

Ediger, Marlow and Digumarti Bhaskara Rao (2000). *Teaching Reading Successfully*. New Delhi: Discovery Publishing House. ISBN 81-7141-556-3.

Ediger, Marlow and Digumarti Bhaskara Rao (2001). *Teaching Science Successfully*. New Delhi: Discovery Publishing House. ISBN 81-7141-600-4.

Ediger, Marlow and Digumarti Bhaskara Rao (2001). *Teaching Social Studies Successfully*. New Delhi: Discovery Publishing House. ISBN 81-7141-596-2.

Ediger, Marlow and Digumarti Bhaskara Rao (2002). *Philosophy and Curriculum*. New Delhi: Discovery Publishing House. ISBN 81-7141-631-4.

Ediger, Marlow and Digumarti Bhaskara Rao (2003). *Improving School Administration*. New Delhi: Discovery Publishing House. ISBN 81-7141-633-0.

Ediger, Marlow and Digumarti Bhaskara Rao (2003). *Elementary Curriculum*. New Delhi: Discovery Publishing House. ISBN 81-7141-658-6.

Ediger, Marlow and Digumarti Bhaskara Rao (2003). *Language Arts Curriculum*. New Delhi: Discovery Publishing House. ISBN 81-7141-657-8.

Ediger, Marlow and Digumarti Bhaskara Rao (2003). *Teaching Language Arts Successfully*. New Delhi: Discovery Publishing House.

Ediger, Marlow, B.S.V. Dutt and Digumarti Bhaskara Rao (2004). *Teaching English Successfully*. New Delhi: Discovery Publishing House.

Jayasree, Kandi and Digumarti Bhaskara Rao, ed. (1999). *Correlates of Socialisation*. New Delhi: Discovery Publishing House. ISBN 81-7141-517-2.

John Babu, Ch., T.J.R. Prasad, G.M. Madhukar and Digumarti Bhaskara Rao, eds. (2001). *Problem Solving in Mathematics*. New Delhi: APH Publishing Corporation. ISBN 81-7648-273-0.

Jyothi, Nirmala and Digumarti Bhaskara Rao, ed. (2002). *Non-Detention System in School Education*. New Delhi: Discovery Publishing House.

Marja, Talvi and Digumarti Bhaskara Rao, eds. (1996). *Educational Leadership and Social Changes*. New Delhi: Discovery Publishing House. ISBN 81-7141-320-X.

Prabhakaram, K.S. and Digumarti Bhaskara Rao, ed. (1998). *Concept Attainment Model in Mathematics Teaching*. New Delhi: Discovery Publishing House. ISBN 81-7141-424-9.

Prasanth Kumar, J. and Digumarti Bhaskara Rao, ed. (1998). *Effectiveness of Distance Education System*. New Delhi: Discovery Publishing House. ISBN 81-7141-437-0.

Prasanth Kumar, J. and Digumarti Bhaskara Rao and G. Sundara Rao ed. (2000). *Open University Student Support Services*. New Delhi: Discovery Publishing House. ISBN 81-7141-550-4.

Ramatulasamma K. and Digumarti Bhaskara Rao, ed. (2002). *Job Satisfaction of Teacher Educators*. New Delhi: Discovery Publishing House.

Ram Krishnaiah, D. and Digumarti Bhaskara Rao, ed. (1998). *Job Satisfaction of College Teachers*. New Delhi: Discovery Publishing House. ISBN 81-7141-438-9.

Ramesh, Ganta and Digumarti Bhaskara Rao, eds. (1998). *Environmental Education: Problems and Prospects*. New Delhi: Discovery Publishing House. ISBN 81-7141-423-0.

Rathaiah, L. and Digumarti Bhaskara Rao, eds. (1997). *International Innovations in Education*. New Delhi: Discovery Publishing House. ISBN 81-7141-359-5.

Rathaiah, Lavu, Digumarti Bhaskara Rao and Paturi Koteswara Rao. (1997). *Achievement Correlates*. New Delhi: Discovery Publishing House. ISBN 81-7141-385-4.

Reddy, Sudhakaray and Digumarti Bhaskara Rao, ed. (2002). *Creativity in Adolescents*. New Delhi: Discovery Publishing House. ISBN 81-7141-659-4.

Sanjeeva Rao, P.C. and Digumarti Bhaskara Rao, ed. (1996). *A Text Book of Geology*. New Delhi: Discovery Publishing House. ISBN 81-7141-313-7.

Satya Narayana, V. and Digumarti Bhaskara Rao, ed. (2001). *Physial Education, Social Attitudes and Leadership Qualities*. New Delhi: Discovery Publishing House. ISBN 81-7141-593-8.

Srinivasulu Reddy, M., K.R.S. Sambasiva Rao and Digumarti Bhaskara Rao, ed. (1999) *A Text Book of Agriculture*. New Delhi: Discovery Publishing House. ISBN 81-7141-482-6.

Vanaja, M. and Digumarti Bhaskara Rao, ed. (1999). *Inquiry Training Model*. New Delhi: Discovery Publishing House. ISBN 81-7141-515-6.

Valeri V. Koustiouk and Digumarti Bhaskara Rao, ed. (2002). *A Text Book of Cryogenics*. New Delhi: Discovery Publishing House. ISBN 81-7141-642-X.

Valeri V. Koustiouk and Digumarti Bhaskara Rao, ed. (2003). *Refrigeration and Environment*. New Delhi: Discovery Publishing House.

Veena Kumari, Balusu and Digumarti Bhaskara Rao (1996). *Operation Black Board*. New Delhi: APH Publishing Corporation. ISBN 81-7024-711-X.

Veena Kumari, B. and Digumarti Bhaskara Rao, ed. (2000). *Psycho-Social Correlates of Achievement*. New Delhi: Discovery Publishing House. ISBN 81-7141-547-4.

Venkata Rao, P. and Digumarti Bhaskara Rao (1989). *A Text Book of Zoology—Junior Intermediate*. Guntur: Vignan Publishers.

Venkata Rao, P. and Digumarti Bhaskara Rao (1989). *A Text Book of Zoology—Senior Intermediate*. Guntur: Vignan Publishers.

Venugopala Rao, K. and Digumarti Bhaskara Rao, ed. (2000). *Teacher Morale in Secondary Schools*. New Delhi: Discovery Publishing House. ISBN 81-7141-551-2.

Vidya, C. and Digumarti Bhaskara Rao, ed. (1996). *A Text Book of Nutrition*. New Delhi: Discovery Publishing House. ISBN 81-7141-309-9.

Vijaya Bharathi, D. and Digumarti Bhaskara Rao, ed. (2000). *Educational Philosophies of Swami Vivekanand and John Dewey*. New Delhi: APH Publishing Corporation. ISBN 81-7648-202-1.

In Telugu Language

Bhaskara Rao, Digumarti. (1996) *Dhrushya Sravana Bodhanapakaranalu* (Audio-Visual Teaching Aids). Guntur: Nagarjuna Publishers.

Bhaskara Rao, Digumarti (1993). *Jeevasashtra Bodhana* (Teaching of Biology). Guntur: Nagarjuna Publishers.

Bhaskara Rao, Digumarti (1995). *Vignanasasthra Bodhana*. (Teaching of Science). Guntur: Nagarjuna Publishers.

Bhaskara Rao, Digumarti (1997). *Vidya Manovignana Sashtram*. (Educational Psychology). Guntur: Creative Press.

Bhaskara Rao, Digumarti (1998). *DSC Study Material*. Guntur: Nagarjuna Publishers.

Bhaskara Rao, Digumarti (1998). *Upadhyayudu Vidya* (Teacher and Education). Guntur: Nagarjuna Publishers.

Bhaskara Rao, Digumarti (1998). *Vidya Dhrukpadhalu*. (Perspectives of Education). Guntur: Nagarjuna Publishers.

Bhaskara Rao, Digumarti (1999). *(EdCET Teaching Aptitude*. Guntur: Nagarjuna Publishers.

Bhasara Rao, Digumarti (2001). *Bharata Samajamulo Upadhayayudu Vidya* (Teacher and Education in Emerging Indian Society). Guntur: Nagarjuna Publishers.

Bhaskara Rao, Digumarti (2001). *Bhoutika Sastra Bodhana Padhatulu* (Methods of Teaching Physical Science). Guntur: Nagarjuna Publishers.

Bhaskara Rao, Digumarti (2001). *Jeeva Sastra Bodhana Padhatulu* (Methods of Teaching Biological Science). Guntur: Nagarjuna Publishers.

Bhaskara Rao, Digumarti (2001). *Vidya Manovignana Sastram* (Educational Psychology). Guntur: Nagarjuna Publishers.